In, Against, and
Beyond Capitalism

KAIROS

In ancient Greek philosophy, *kairos* signifies the right time or the "moment of transition." We believe that we live in such a transitional period. The most important task of social science in time of transformation is to transform itself into a force of liberation. Kairos, an editorial imprint of the Anthropology and Social Change department housed in the California Institute of Integral Studies, publishes groundbreaking works in critical social sciences, including anthropology, sociology, geography, theory of education, political ecology, political theory, and history.

Series editor: Andrej Grubačić

Kairos books:

In, Against, and Beyond Capitalism: The San Francisco Lectures by John Holloway

Anthropocene or Capitalocene? Nature, History, and the Crisis of Capitalism edited by Jason W. Moore

Birth Work as Care Work: Stories from Activist Birth Communities by Alana Apfel

Wrapped in the Flag of Israel: Mizrahi Single Mothers, Israeli Ultra-Nationalism, and Bureaucratic Torture by Smadar Lavie

We Are the Crisis of Capital: A John Holloway Reader by John Holloway

In, Against, and Beyond Capitalism

The San Francisco Lectures

John Holloway

KAIROS

PM

In, Against, and Beyond Capitalism: The San Francisco Lectures
John Holloway
© 2016 PM Press.

ISBN: 978-1-62963-109-7
Library of Congress Control Number: 2015930910

Cover by John Yates / www.stealworks.com
Interior design by briandesign

10 9 8 7 6 5 4 3 2 1

PM Press
PO Box 23912
Oakland, CA 94623
www.pmpress.org

Printed in the USA by the Employee Owners of Thomson-Shore in Dexter, Michigan.
www.thomsonshore.com

Contents

Why Holloway?

To criticize positive thinking is a dangerous thing in California, particularly if you do it in a room called Namaste Hall. Yet, in these three delightful lectures delivered at the California Institute of Integral Studies in April 2013, that is precisely what John Holloway did. Students and activists cheered him on, disagreed, and actively participated in one of the more memorable intellectual exchanges organized by the Department of Anthropology and Social Change.

In this preface, I will discuss the nature of John Holloway's Marxism and its place in contemporary anticapitalist theory. I will focus on four key areas in Holloway's thinking.

The first one is dialectics. As Roy Bhaskar and critical realists have pointed out (Norries 2009), the entire Western philosophical tradition can be explained as a confrontation between two very different positions. The first position, introduced by Parmenides, insists on apparent fixity of objects. Objects are fixed and protected from change. The other, Heraclitean, position sees objects as patterns of change (Graeber 2001). The world is a constant flux, bereft of solid objects. For Holloway, as for Adorno, "thinking heeds a potential that waits in the object." Objects, or constitutive elements, are in constant motion, and our thought resists to "mere things in being" (Adorno 1990: 19). The best-known examples of thought that sees objects as processes and society as constituted by action are Hegel and Marx. It would be accurate enough to state that Holloway stands firmly in dialectical tradition, and he indeed patiently argues that it is theoretically and politically important to defend the notion of dialectics. It would be, at the same time, equally inaccurate to stop there. Holloway's dialectics is not Hegel's, and his political and intellectual project is defined by an effort to develop a notion of open and *negative* dialectics.

After the defeat of the real existing socialism, many Marxists, particularly those in the French-speaking world, have rejected the dogmatic certainty of the positive thought. No more synthetic thinking, they declared, no more closure, no more certainty. This reaction was entirely reasonable, as it was an intellectual and political protest against the official thought of the French communist party. The new generation of post-1968 Marxists, including Deleuze, Guattari, Foucault, and Negri, made what seemed a reasonable move from Hegel to Spinoza, a move from contradiction to difference. This poststructuralist current jettisoned coherent totalities, abstract categories, and monolithic revolutionary subjects. In doing so, Holloway argues, they went too far, throwing the proverbial baby out with the bathwater. As Holloway is quick to point out, their intellectual anxiety is perfectly justified when one deals with unitary, or positive synthesis, and when the famous "contradiction" is embodied in the positive concept of the working class. The great paradox, he went on to argue in several important books (Holloway 2005 and 2010), is that extremism in rejecting dialectics led these same theorists to a new positivation of thought, and to a return to a synthetic closure. The new autonomist or post-workerist theory that has emerged with the antiglobalization movement, best represented in the works of Antonio Negri, Michael Hardt, and Colectivo Situaciones, identified all dialectics with the synthetic, Hegelian tradition. This, in turn, has serious political consequences. Instead of an open-ended thinking that celebrates the most important insight of Marx—the idea that the world consists of processes and actions, rather than of discrete and separable objects—this new positivism has embraced new totalities ("Empire" and "multitude"), lending support to political parties and socialist governments.

This is why, instead of rejecting dialectic thinking, Holloway invites us to redefine and develop it further. His Marxism is premised on another form of logic, one that affirms movement, instability, and struggle. This is a movement of thought that affirms the richness of life, particularity (non-identity) and "walking in the opposite direction"; walking, that is, away from exploitation, domination, and classification. Without contradictory thinking in, against, and beyond the capitalist society, capital once again becomes a reified object, a thing, and not a social relation that signifies transformation of a useful and creative activity (doing) into (abstract) labor. Only open dialectics, a right kind of thinking for the wrong kind of world, non-unitary thinking without guarantees, is able to assist us in our contradictory struggle for a world free of contradiction.

The second area of influence in Holloway's work is Italian autonomist thought in general, and Mario Tronti in particular. In his seminal article "Lenin in England" (1979), Tronti wrote, "We too have worked with a concept that puts capitalist development first, and workers second. This is a mistake. And now we have to put the problem on its head, reverse the polarity, and start again from the beginning: and the beginning is the class struggle of the working class" (1979: 1). This famous inversion of the capital-labor relation defined the early autonomist project. In order to understand capitalism, the argument goes, we have to start from the struggles of the working class. Capitalism develops in the constant movement of composition-decomposition-recomposition. This implies that new forms of social organization are not inevitable results of unfolding capitalist rationality. The problem here, Holloway argues, is that for many of the post-autonomist thinkers, including Antonio Negri (Hardt and Negri 2000; 2004) and Paulo Virno (2004), the Trontian inversion is lost. Without negative thinking, these theorists have developed a paradigmatic approach that focuses on analysis of domination. This, in Holloway's view, is *positive autonomism*. This is Marxism as a theory of restructuring of capitalism, not Marxism as a theory of crisis. The new revolutionary agent, the multitude, is an identitarian subject, deduced from relations of domination. Thus, Holloway calls for *negative autonomism* and revolutionary analysis that is not static and frozen in the world of abstract labor.

The Trontian inversion is extremely important in opening of the Marxist canon, but it only goes halfway. The other half is provided by Adorno's *Negative Dialectics* (1990). This might sound a bit strange. John Holloway is known for his boundless, infectious optimism and dreamy revolutionary prose. He is never removed from social and political struggle, always inspecting the world for cracks in the world of capital and domination. Adorno, on the other hand, is usually regarded as a cultural elitist: the epitome of a resigned philosopher, a pessimistic theorist with a notoriously opaque style, and an unfortunate habit of calling police on his students. For Holloway, however, the theoretical legacy of Theodor Adorno is more layered and nuanced. Adorno makes it possible to build a revolutionary theory that puts the concept and movement of non-identity (particularity) first. It is not enough to put the working class in place of capital and leave identity intact. It is here that negative or critical thought reveals itself as indispensible. Negative dialectics is the ontology of the wrong state of things. "The right state of things would be free of it: neither a system nor a contradiction." (1990: 11).

Adorno's intention is to "use the strength of the subject to break through the fallacy of constituted subjectivity—this is what the author felt to be his task ever since he came to trust his own mental impulses" (1990: xx). Dialectics is struggle against identity, a misfitting logic for a negative subject that exist in, against, and beyond capital. Liberated from positivist heritage, dialectics is negation without synthesis, a creative movement against identity, an overflowing of thought that puts non-identity at the center of analysis: "dialectics is the consistent sense of non-identity." This is the (second) key element in Holloway's thinking. The working class rebels against capitalism—it constitutes the crisis of capitalism—but also against itself. This open political subject, the working class, becomes an inclusive and contradictory "we," a creative force with "a consistent sense of non-identity." Thinking against (constituted subjectivity) and doing against (alienated labor) refuses identity and understands class struggle as permanent negative revolution: an explosion of human creativity (what we hope Marx really wanted to capture by that much contested term "forces of production"). Revolutionary theory is, then, a critique of the very essence of bourgeois thought, a critique leveled against those categories of political economy that conceal the antagonism between abstract labor and creative (contradictory) human doing. With the help of Adorno, the inversion is complete. Tronti needs the negativity of Adorno, and Adorno is incomplete without the creativity of Tronti. There is no consistent autonomism without critical theory, and no effective critical theory without the autonomist project at its core (Holloway, Matamoros, and Tischler 2009).

The third theoretical influence in Holloway's writing is the state derivationist argument. Perhaps the least known of all participants in the rich world of Marxist state debates of the 1970s, the German state derivationist school played an important role in Holloway's intellectual formation. Holloway and Picciotto (1978) were the first Marxists to introduce this important theoretical current to the English-speaking world. The main derivationist thesis was that the central question in any debate on the state must be the form that the state takes ("form analysis"). The autonomy of the state is illusion, as the state does not stand outside and independent from capital and processes of accumulation. States are relations and organizational forms created for reproduction of capital. The great theoretical contribution of the derivationist school was to remind Marxists that any approach to the state must be "based on the dialectic of the form and content of class struggle" (1978: 31). Holloway was influenced particularly by Joachim Hirsch's emphasis on the state as a capitalist form of social relations. The political conclusion Holloway took from this was that, if the state is indeed a capitalist form of social relations, then you can't think of using it to bring about revolution. The state is, as Holloway defines it in this book, a specific form of social organization, a way of doing and seeing things, a form of social organization that excludes people. States, even when they are "pink," have a dual effect on social movements: they separate the leadership from movement, and they draw movements into a process of reconciliation with capital. This is why state-centered politics needs to be abandoned and replaced by the "anti-grammar of revolution." This conviction received new impulse after Holloway's move to Mexico and, especially, after the Zapatista uprising.

In January 1994, on the day the North American Free Trade Agreement (NAFTA) between Mexico, Canada, and the United States took effect, a group of Maya indigenous people declared war on the Mexican government and seized several municipalities in the southern state of Chiapas. In the First Declaration of the Lacandon Jungle released on the day of the uprising, the Zapatista Army of National Liberation (EZLN) expressed their demands: work, land, housing, food, health, education, independence, liberty, democracy, justice, and peace. They cited Article 39 of the Mexican Constitution: "the people have, at all times, the inalienable right to change or modify the form of their government." As the Mexican military moved to suppress the uprising, millions of people around the world demanded that the army end its attack on the Zapatistas. The EZLN withdrew from municipal headquarters but the land they occupied became "territory in rebellion." They eschewed violence yet remained a guerrilla force committed to "autonomy": territorial self-organization and self-administration of politics, justice, education, health, and economy.

John Holloway was one of the first to recognize the significance of the Zapatistas' reinvention of politics (Holloway and Pelaez 1998). While Negri and other positive autonomists looked for a new revolutionary proletariat in the "cognitariat," those "immaterial" workers tinkering with the internet in the core countries of the world-system, Holloway insisted that the new politics is being forged by the indigenous campesinos in Chiapas. The Zapatistas have refused traditional tenets of socialist developmentalism, including state-centered politics and Leninist vanguardism. In Holloway's view, Zapatistas present an example of a "dialogical politics." They have made their dictum "preguntando caminamos" (asking, we walk) the central principle of creative self-activity. The old certainties and tired dogmatism are thrown out. What emerges is *Zapatismo*, not an ideology as much as a festival of ideas. This is not an incoherent but profoundly *contradictory* set of ideas and practices. This, more then anything else, is what inspires Holloway. The very heart of Zapatismo is a contradiction between a form of organization (they are, after all, an army) and the movement of insubordination (they are an army that aspires not to be one). Contradiction is particularly pronounced in the contrast between the military structure of the organization and the autonomous modes of life in the indigenous communities. Zapatistas are not a synthesis; resistance is not reduced to a positive figure. They say, "We are ordinary people, we are perfectly ordinary women and men, children and old people, and that is why we are rebellious." This contradictory politics includes an interesting relationship to collective identity. Zapatistas (ref)use identity. They have said from the beginning, "We are a movement which is almost totally indigenous in composition, but we are not just an indigenous movement. We are not just fighting for indigenous rights, we are actually fighting for humanity." Escaping classification, Zapatismo is a constant movement of *dignified fury*. Finally, Zapatistas inhabit a territory or, to use Holloway's terms, a spatial "crack." For thirty years, in the jungles and mountains of Chiapas, Zapatistas have developed a society built on different sort of social relations, an elaborate form of social organization distinct from the logic of the state. In the Zapatista areas of Chiapas, you pass a sign that says "Bad Government Stay Out, Here the People Rule."

Let me try to bring some of these ideas together. Holloway's Marxism is a creative and original combination of insights from state derivationism, autonomist tradition, critical theory, and Zapatismo. Just like other Marxisms, he begins with forces and relations of production, but these are defined rather differently from the ones I had to memorize in my school subjects in socialist Yugoslavia. Communism is not about big tractors and assembly lines. It is a society that is always reinventing, created on the basis of human creativity and self-determination. The forces of productions are people themselves. This is why Holloway refuses to begin with capital and domination, or with the "miserable pit of commodity." Just like other Marxisms, he speaks of class. But this class does not consist, at least not exclusively, of male factory workers. It is a class that rebels against capitalist society and against itself, a revolutionary subject against identity. Working class is movement against work, or against alienated labor and identitarian classification. We are "the movement that breaks the cohesion, that breaks the synthesis, that breaks identities." Our infinite diversity is the principal basis of our solidarity. Capitalism is a system of deadly but weak social cohesion based on abstract labor, predicated on the dual process of *abstraction* of our creative doing into labor, and of *classification* of our richness into identities. This is, according to Holloway, the best-kept secret of capitalism and its central weakness. Capitalism is a deadly but tortured synthesis, an oppressive dynamic that is always in crisis. It has to be in crisis as it depends on us, on our labor, on the value we produce, and on our participation.

In keeping with the anarchist and councilist tradition, Holloway cautions against the state/party-option. He advocates a "crack-option" instead, "the outcome of the barely visible transformation of the daily activities of millions of people," and located "beyond activism" in "millions of cracks that constitute the material base of possible radical change" (2010: 12). Is he a revolutionary? Most definitely. But the role of the revolution is not to replace one totality with another; the revolutionary task is to break the dynamic of capital. Revolution is imagined as a double movement, negative and creative, an interstitial movement that creates cracks in the texture of domination. These cracks are spaces-in-movement, moments (not institutions!) of alternative creation. There are at least three types of cracks. They can be spatial (Zapatistas are always a good example), temporal (refusal of 24/7 capitalism, appropriation of time and autonomous elaboration of associated activities), or structural (activities that promote non-monetized, non-commodified social relations). We should not take the state, we should crack it. If we think of revolution not in terms of conquering fortresses and palaces, but in terms of *deepening* the cracks, the most important question before us is how we can promote the multiplication and convergence of these self-governed organizational forms. Holloway's recommendation is to "keep building cracks and finding ways of recognizing them, strengthening them, expanding them, connecting them; seeking the confluence or, preferably, the commoning of the cracks." This might sound too hazy or dreamy to those using the conventional "grammar of revolution." The problem, however, is that after several centuries of a catastrophic obsession with taking state power, this conventional language sounds not only less poetic but also far less realistic.

As I write this preface, I remember the last time my compañera and I met with John at his home in Puebla. He was kind enough to show us his favorite place, his most cherished crack: an autonomous garden maintained by his compañera and a group of enthusiastic students. Rarely have I seen a place of such magnificent beauty. "This is where I wrote *Crack Capitalism*," he told us, pointing to a table surrounded by flowers, in the shadow of a big, luscious tree. Here we spent hours discussing Syriza and Podemos, progressive political forces in Europe that he supports. But he hastens to add that what he is really afraid of is massive disappointment when these parties fail to deliver their promise. "These are serious people," he says, "but the form of struggle they have chosen is wrong." These conversations were fresh in my mind when we returned to the Bay Area. In the aftermath of Occupy Oakland, everything seems so confusing: Who is the revolutionary subject? How do we reach out to the workers? Should we occupy or decolonize? Do we need to riot or to check our privilege? Should we support Bernie Sanders? Activists are discussing bad choices and less-worse choices. Encounter and experiment are, at least for the moment, replaced by habit and identity.

Why Holloway, then?[1]

That's why.

References

Adorno, Theodor W. *Negative Dialectics*. London: Routledge, 1990.

Graeber, David. *Toward an Anthropological Theory of Value: The False Coin of Our Own Dreams*. London: Palgrave Macmillan, 2001.

Hardt, Michael, and Antonio Negri. *Empire*. Cambridge, MA: Harvard University Press, 2000.

Hardt, Michael, and Antonio Negri. *Multitude*. New York, Penguin Books, 2004.

Holloway, John. *Change the World Without Taking Power: The Meaning of Revolution Today*. London: Pluto, 2005.

Holloway, John. *Crack Capitalism*. London: Pluto, 2010.

---

1   The title and conclusion "Why Holloway?" is a playful reference to Holloway's chapter "Why Adorno?" in John Holloway, Fernando Matamoros, and Sergio Tischler, eds., *Negativity and Revolution: Adorno and Political Activism*.

Holloway, John, Fernando Matamoros, and Sergio Tischler, eds. *Negativity and Revolution: Adorno and Political Activism*. London: Pluto, 2009.

Holloway, John, and Eleina Pelaez, eds. *Zapatista! Reinventing Revolution in Mexico*. London: Pluto Press, 1998.

Holloway, John, and Sol Picciotto. *State and Capital: A Marxist Debate*. London: E. Arnold, 1978.

Norries, Allan. *Dialectic and Difference: Dialectical Critical Realism and the Grounds of Justice*. London: Routledge, 2009.

Tronti, Mario. "Lenin in England." In *Working Class Autonomy and the Crisis: Italian Marxist Texts of the Theory and Practice of a Class Movement, 1964–79*. London: Red Notes, 1979.

Virno, Paulo. *A Grammar of the Multitude: For an Analysis of Contemporary Forms of Life*. New York: Semiotext(e), 2004.

ONE

Who Are We?

Whenever I come to a new place I always feel slightly nervous, because I'm not quite sure where you are. I've got a rough idea of where I am, but I'm never quite sure where everybody else is. And this is only the third time that I've ever come to speak in the Evil Empire itself. I feel it's a process of exploration, by which I hope we will be able to find one another over the next few days. But it may well be that what I say is just pushing through open doors or is absolutely, totally incomprehensible or just irrelevant. So, if you want to interrupt me, or boo, or applaud wildly from time to time, then please feel free to do so.

I know roughly where I want to go. We've got three sessions. What I want to say at the end is "We Are the Crisis of Capital and Proud of It." It seems to me that that is fundamentally important politically, but that's at the end. I'm not going to get there this evening.

What I want to do this evening is start, start at the beginning. If I say where I want to go is "We Are the Crisis of Capital," then clearly the beginning is "We." What I want to talk about is simply that, We.

We, because I think the starting point is very important. More and more I think that where we start, where we start talking or where we start a conversation or where we start writing an essay or where we start writing a thesis really has a fundamental effect on what follows. And the great tradition, the great Marxist tradition certainly, is to start not with We, not with Us, but with Them. With capital. With talking about capitalist domination, the changing forms of capitalist domination. This seems to me absolutely disastrous. It seems to me disastrous because I think that the starting point locks us in. If we start from capital, we then go on to try and elaborate a theory of domination. And by elaborating a theory of domination we are actually closing ourselves in. It's a great tradition on the Left to say that if we talk about domination in this beautiful, free, liberal society we live in—if we say it's not really a free and liberal society, it's really a society based on capitalist domination—that is in some way progressive, that we're moving forward in some way. I think that's not true at all, for two reasons.

First, because it's perfectly obvious that we live in a society based on domination. It's perfectly obvious that we live in a nasty, oppressive, capitalist society. That's not really the problem, that's a prescientific statement. It's after that that the problem starts. It's after that you have to start thinking, "Fine, of course we do, but how on earth do we get out of it?" That's the issue, I think. The danger is that if we start with domination we actually lock ourselves into elaborating a theory of domination and we set the framework within which we ourselves think. We first elaborate a theory of domination and then, afterwards, we start to talk about social struggle or class struggle. And I don't think that works, so I don't want to start from that. I don't want to start from the nasties, I want to start from We, who are lovely.

We could start, of course, from the working class. We could say, "We are the proletariat, the working class." But I'm not going to do that either, at least not for the moment. Maybe we will get to it. I'm not going to do it for the moment, first because it seems to me formulaic, if that's the word. It leads us into thinking in terms of formulas. If we start saying, "We have to break capitalism, obviously, therefore we have to start from the working class, who are us," then I think we get into old formulas, and the old formulas don't work. I want to come back to the question of the working class, but not actually to start from there.

The other great danger about starting from the working class is that it very easily becomes a third-person discourse. We start thinking about the working class as They. The whole revolutionary, and certainly the whole Leninist tradition thinks of the working class as a They. They are the revolutionary subject. How can we think about realizing the revolutionary potential of a Them? The problem if you start thinking about Them is you start getting into a politics that treats the Them as an object in some way. You start getting into a politics of thinking on behalf of the Them. Anyway, we can come back to that as well. What I want to say is that we have to start with Us.

Who are We? What does We mean? I think it's important because I think there is a shift . . . what I hope we will be talking about in these three sessions is a shift in the grammar of anticapitalism—a shift in the way we think about anticapitalism and a shift in the forms of anticapitalist action. One of the aspects of that change of grammar is that anticapitalist movements, more and more, are talking about themselves as We. They don't talk so much about the working class or the downtrodden or the marginalized or whatever. More and more, the key figure is We. And if we ask who is We or, if we want to be a bit more grammatical, who are We, then we come quickly to the idea that We are a Question. We don't actually know very well. It's not a predefined category, it's an open We, it's a We that invites, that provokes. It's a We that asks: Who are We?

The title of these talks is After Capitalism. I suppose, to be honest, I'm not quite sure what After Capitalism means. But I suppose it means, in the first place, anticapitalism. We can perhaps say that most of us here, or probably all of us, are anticapitalist. And then we can ask why are we anticapitalist. Until about three days ago I thought the answer was obvious. I thought, well, of course we're anticapitalist because capitalism stinks! We're anticapitalist because capitalism is a disaster for humanity. We're anticapitalist because if we don't break capitalism, if we don't change the system in some way, then it is very likely that the dynamic of this system will lead to the total destruction of humanity. Of course we're anticapitalist. But it struck me then that there is one little step missing in that argument. Capitalism is a disastrous system, an authoritarian system, a horrible system, therefore we are against it. But then you begin to think of bees, you begin to think of ants. Bees and ants, they live in a horrible, authoritarian system as well, where everything is predefined and where there is a hierarchy but, at least as far as I know, bees and ants don't rebel against the hierarchy of their hives and their nests. So it doesn't follow automatically from the fact that the system is nasty that therefore we rise up against it. The point that's missing is that there must be something that distinguishes us. It's not that I have anything against bees or ants, not at all. I hold them in a lot of respect, but there must be something else. We must be different in some way from bees and ants. That leads us to the first point I want to suggest.

We is a question. We have enough experience to suggest answers, answers that are also questions or perhaps provocations. The first thing, I suppose, that distinguishes us from ants and bees is that We are dignity. We revolt, We rebel against the negation of our dignity. And I'm going to quote, because it's one of my favorite quotes and you probably all know it, or you should all know it by heart and be able to quote it without thinking, but all the same I'm going to quote it because it's so beautiful. From one of the early Zapatista letters, the letter from the Zapatista clandestine committee to another indigenous organization, written right at the start of the uprising, just at the end of January 1994, in which they explain why they rose up. They say:

> Then that suffering that united us made us speak, and we
> recognized that, in our words, there was truth. We knew

that not only pain and suffering lived in our tongue. We recognized that there is hope still in our hearts. We spoke with ourselves, we looked inside ourselves and we looked at our history: we saw our most ancient fathers suffering and struggling, we saw our grandfathers struggling, we saw our fathers with fury in their hands, we saw that not everything had been taken away from us, that we had the most valuable, that which made us live, that which made our step rise above plants and animals, that which made the stone be beneath our feet, and we saw, brothers, that all that we had was *dignity*, and we saw that great was the shame of having forgotten it, and we saw that *dignity* was good for men to be men again, and dignity returned to live in our hearts, and we were new again, and the dead, our dead, saw that we were new again, and they called us again to dignity, to struggle.

So, if we're anticapitalist it's not just that capitalism stinks, it's also that we're saying something about ourselves, we are saying that We have dignity or We are dignity. To say We are dignified in English doesn't sound right, so we say We are dignity. We are dignity and therefore we will not accept the world that we are born into. Therefore we will not accept this world of destruction, this world of disaster. What we will not accept, at the end of the day, is the negation of our own dignity. We will not accept. So, dignity is negated, but it is not entirely negated, because if it were entirely negated then it would be impossible for us to have a concept of dignity. Dignity is enraged. Our dignity is enraged. This is the place from where We start, probably the place from where we all start in this room, a position of enraged dignity, of dignified fury, of *digna rabia*, as the Zapatistas call it.

There are lots of ways of thinking about dignity. One way of thinking of it is Here We Are. Here we are as subjects. The world tells us that we are not here, that we really don't matter.

In the world that we see on the television, the world that we read about in the papers, we're not there. We are the invisible. Dignity is the invisible making themselves visible. It is the Zapatistas putting on their balaclavas, their ski helmets, so that they can be seen, covering their faces so that people can see them. Dignity is the dignity of the invisible, it is the dignity of the latent, but the dignity of the latent that is in movement. Dignity is volcanic, it is that which moves beneath the surface, it is that which brings us here tonight.

We are not victims, that is surely the important point about dignity. When we talk about dignity we are saying no, no way are we victims; we will not start from being victims. If we think of ourselves as being victims, then we are lost. If we start from a world of domination then we start by defining ourselves as victims, as being the bearers of the relations of domination. And it's not that. We are not victims, and We are not poor either. The great Left tradition is "oh dear oh dear, poor us, poor us, we suffer so much." Well it's not that. It's not that. Because if we start from that, in a way we kill ourselves from the beginning. It's not that we are poor, that's not why we rise up, why we protest. It's not because we're poor, it's because we're rich. The starting point surely for our rebelliousness is not poverty, it is actually richness. I think it's important to say that. It's not that we start off from being poor, we start off from being rich. Marx, it seems to me, says that very clearly. If you think of how *Capital* starts, the first sentence of *Capital* is "The wealth of those societies in which the capitalist mode of production prevails appears as 'an immense accumulation of commodities.'" And everybody says, literally without exception, that Marx starts his analysis from the commodity. But in fact he doesn't. If you think of that first sentence, he starts off with the wealth, he starts from our richness. He doesn't start from our defeat, from our depravity, from our deformation. He actually starts from our richness. And there's a beautiful passage—I'm going to quote that as well. I'm into quoting things this evening, sorry. There's a beautiful passage from the *Grundrisse*, where Marx explains what he means by richness. He says, "In fact, however, when the limited bourgeois form is stripped away," in other words when the commodity form is stripped away, "what is wealth other than the universality of human needs, capacities, pleasures, productive forces, etc., created through universal exchange? … The absolute working out of [humanity's] creative potentialities with no presupposition other than the previous historical development, which makes this totality of development, that is the development of all human powers as such, the end in itself. Not as measured on a predetermined yardstick? Where he does not produce himself in one specificity but produces his totality? Strives not to remain something he has become, but is in the absolute movement of becoming?" This is so beautiful!

That's where he starts. He starts from this richness and then falls into this miserable pit of the commodity. That's what it's all about. And then we read it and we forget about the first bit of the sentence and we think, "Oh yes, he's starting with the commodity." He's not! We do it ourselves, we start from domination and we think that's what it is. No, we shouldn't. Let's start from ourselves, let's start from ourselves and from our own richness.

We Are the Only Gods. We are the only creators. We are the only creators, at least of our own society. We are the creators of the wealth on which capital depends. The lords always depend on their servants. The masters always depend on their slaves, that is the source of hope. One more quotation, which is also a favorite and it's going to be my last quotation because that's enough! This is a quotation from the sixteenth-century French theorist La Boétie, who says, addressing the people, in his *Discourse on Voluntary Servitude*:

> You sow your crops in order that he [the lord] may ravage them; you install and furnish your homes to give him goods to pillage; you rear your daughters that

he may gratify his lust; you bring up your children in order that he may confer upon them the greatest privilege he knows—to be led into his battles, to be delivered to butchery, to be made the servants of his greed and the instruments of his vengeance; you yield your bodies unto hard labor in order that he may indulge in his delights and wallow in his filthy pleasures; you weaken yourselves in order to make him the stronger and the mightier to hold you in check. From all these indignities, such as the very beasts of the field would not endure, you can deliver yourselves if you try, not by taking action, but merely by willing to be free. Resolve to serve no more, and you are at once freed. I do not ask that you place hands upon the tyrant to topple him over, but simply that you support him no longer; then you will behold him, like a great Colossus whose pedestal has been pulled away, fall of his own weight and break in pieces.

This is beautiful! This is beautiful and sounds very simple and perhaps it isn't so simple, but the point is basic, the point is fundamental, the point is that the rulers always depend upon the ruled. And that is our strength and that is our hope. Of course, it is not just La Boétie, that's also Hegel's argument if you think of the master-servant dialectic. But, also, it is Marx's argument: that is what the labor theory of value is about! The economists have captured the labor theory of value and made us think that it is a theory about how the economy works. But the basic thing about the labor theory of value is to say that capital depends upon the value that is produced by the people it dominates. In other words, capital depends upon labor.

We Are the Center of the World. We are the center of the world and We are in rebellion. That's why we're here tonight, because we are in rebellion in one sense or another. And we are in rebellion because we are ordinary. That, as well, seems

8

to me very important. We are in rebellion not because we are special. Obviously we could think, "Well, here we are tonight, I don't know how many people but let's say sixty or so—we are special." Outside, in San Francisco, there are so many people that didn't come. I don't quite understand why not, but we could think, "Well, we're special but they're not special." That, again, seems to me part of the Left tradition. But, once we say that, we're finished. Once we say that, then the only way in which we can think about revolution or radical change is as an elitist movement. Once we say we are special, then we are actually enclosing ourselves into an elitist concept of social change, or else just complete pessimism. The most exciting and the most difficult and the most challenging thing that the Zapatistas say, to come back to them again, is when they say. "We are ordinary people, we are perfectly ordinary women and men, children and old people, and that is why we are rebellious." That seems to me amazingly challenging. They're not saying, "We are ordinary indigenous people in the southeast of Mexico." They're not saying that, they won't let you away with any romanticism. It's not Them, it's not the indigenous, it's not the people who look a little bit different who are going to save us. No, they're not saying that, they're saying, "We are ordinary people." The challenge then is to try and think that, not just looking at the person beside you in the room and thinking, "Oh well, if they're here tonight it's because they are rebels too." It means going out to the street afterwards and trying to see the rebellion inside people. And it means going to the shops or going to the supermarket—the next time you go and see that quiet old man there choosing his cornflakes or whatever—and recognizing the rebelliousness in them. If we can't do that, then we're lost. That's the real challenge, it seems to me.

The challenge of thinking of our revolt or of our rebelliousness as being ordinary is also the challenge of dignity, which is really the challenge of the mutual recognition of dignities. Because if we just say, "We are dignity, not the people outside, poor masses; We are dignity." If we say that, then it's nonsense. The very notion of dignity means trying to recognize the dignity of ordinary people. It means trying to recognize the rebelliousness of ordinary people, It means trying to find a practical recognition of dignity, which leads us to a certain concept of politics. It must lead to a certain concept of politics, because then it means that we are trying to think of political organization in a way that will articulate dignities.

If we think of the whole anticapitalist tradition right back to the beginning, I suppose we've really got to separate ways of thinking about it and two sorts of thinking about organization. One tradition is the tradition of councils, of assemblies, of soviets, the tradition that, in order to move forward in-against-and-beyond this world which denies our dignity, which denies our subjectivity, we have to be able to build forms of organization that express that which is negated in the actual world. In other words, we have to build forms of organization that allow people to articulate their dignities, that encourage people to speak, that encourage people to explain their worries, that encourage people to talk about their concerns, that encourage people to draw out their dignity. I think that's been a fantastic thing about the whole Occupy movement, the whole *indignados* movement, and the whole movement in North Africa and all over the place. For the last couple of years at least, there has been an overwhelming movement of "assemblyism." It is truly a revival of that tradition of councilism, which seems to me enormously important.

The other tradition is to think that if we want to bring about change, then we must think instrumentally. We must think of the most effective way of bringing about changes, which means that, at least in the short term, we must enter into the power structures established by society. We must, in other words, get involved with the state; we must think of political parties; we must think, at least, of political pressure groups. Which means we try and think of going into the state in order to try and bring about change and that means getting involved in forms of organization that are hierarchical, getting involved in forms of organization that deny and run counter to the mutual recognition of dignities. It may well be that these forms of organization can bring about changes in the short term, or at least small changes, but they don't actually break the dynamic of the society in which we live. They don't break the dynamic of death.

You can think, if you like, of the contrast between the politics of dignity and the politics of poverty. The politics of poverty starts, as I said a few minutes ago, not from richness but from the poor. OK, here we are, here, in the university institution, we're not desperately poor. But outside, yes, outside it's amazing, it's been hitting me all day today, the amount of poverty in the streets of San Francisco, it's just appalling. And then you begin to think, "Yes, of course we have to change that. We have to change society on behalf of the poor." And then you get into a different logic, a different way of thinking about social change, a different way of thinking about radical change. You get into a politics of poverty, which may achieve things. You could argue that in Venezuela, Bolivia, Brazil, Argentina, yes, it has achieved changes. But it also reproduces the whole system. Because once you think of people as poor, once you think of the politics of poverty, then you try to change things on behalf of people. In other words, you're making them the object of your action. And the problem with that is that often people say, "Well, we don't want to be the object of what you think." So, I think it's important to make that distinction between a politics of poverty and a politics of dignity. They really lead us in different directions.

Another thing about us is that We exist in, against, and beyond this society. We exist in this society, because this is where we live, where we have to survive. This is where we have to find a way of making a living, a way of reproducing ourselves, of looking after the people we love. But We also exist against it, because We know what an awful society it is, we know what a disaster it is, so We exist in and against this society. And We also exist beyond, because, all the time, what We are trying to do is to create ways of relating to other people that don't follow the logic of money, that don't follow the capitalist pattern. We're trying to do something else, trying to walk in the wrong direction, trying to say no, that's not right, We're going to do something else. We're going to create that something else. It can be all sorts of things. It can be organizing talks on anticapitalism, trying to teach students to be critical. It can be creating different relations with the plants and other forms of life that surround us. It can be creating gardens, it can be doing all sorts of things. There are millions of ways doing it. All the time—and this is something I'll get back to later on—all the time we're creating cracks in the logic of the system that dominates us.

But if we're creating cracks, that also means that we are self-antagonistic. Because We don't live just beyond the society. We don't live in some kind of after-capitalist heaven, unfortunately. We live in this society and also live against it. We try to create something else which means that We are inevitably self-antagonistic, in some sense turned against ourselves, that We are inevitably schizophrenic, in the popular sense of being self-divided, not in a clinical sense. If we start thinking of that, then one notion goes out the window completely and that is the notion of revolutionary purity. The notion of revolutionary purity, the notion that we are correct but those poor ignorant masses over there don't know how to do things properly—once we start with that, we destroy ourselves. And that's another of the great Left traditions: let's all kill ourselves through sectarianism. The police don't come into it very much; we can destroy ourselves perfectly well, thank you. The very fact that We live with dignity against the denial of dignity means inevitably that We are self-contradictory. Once we think that, then we can say, "OK, yes, we don't have the perfect answer. They don't either, those people over there don't either," and we can certainly criticize them. We can certainly say we don't agree with where they are going, we think it would be much more effective to go some other way, but we cannot criticize them from the point of view of correctness. We can only criticize them from the point of view of trying to find more effective or better ways of expressing our repudiation of the system.

We are self-contradictory, and this seems to me important. We rebel because We misfit. The dictionary tells me that misfit is a noun and not a verb, but too bad for the dictionary. We actually misfit, We don't fit in. Again, if we are here tonight it is because we have some sense of misfitting. We don't fit into the classifications, into the patterns that capitalism seems to put on us. And again, if we go back to the first sentence of *Capital*, where wealth appears in capitalist society as an immense collection of commodities, it seems to me that Marx is saying wealth does not fit into that. It's true! The commodification of wealth is a structural misfitting. The whole idea is that commodity or capital is a procrustean bed, one that forces us into a certain shape. Only it doesn't work! It doesn't work because if it did work we would be incapable of seeing that that is what is happening. We fall out over the edges of this rack or bed in one way or another. We misfit, this is what constitutes our dignity. What constitutes our rebelliousness is that We don't fit into the classifications. We're misfits, not because we're weirdos necessarily. We're misfits because capitalism misfits us, because capitalism forces us into shapes in which we cannot fit. So We necessarily misfit.

And that means that We are anti-identitarian. It means that We don't fit into identities. I don't know if identity politics started in San Francisco—I suspect that it did! But the problem with identity politics is that it tends to fit everything into classifications and we don't! This is of fundamental importance—We don't fit in! The basis of our dignity, the basis of our rebelliousness is that We don't fit into classifications, into little boxes. We can say, as I think the Zapatistas do, We are indigenous but more than that. We can say We are gay but more than that. We are women but are more than that, or We are Irish but more than that. But if we don't say that "but more than that," then it becomes reactionary. It becomes a conservative statement; it becomes the creation of a new category. And capital, I think, has absolutely no problem with creating spaces for new boxes. No problem at all. What capital cannot cope with is the overflowing, the going beyond categories, the misfitting, the conscious misfitting which says yes, We misfit, and We are proud of it.

We misfit, We are anti-identitarian and therefore anti-institutional as well. Institutionalization is a way of classifying, a way of closing. There is a debate going on at the moment about what the Left should be doing, what the movements of anti-globalization, what We should be doing after the whole wave of movements over the last few years and there is an argument that we should think in terms of creating new institutions. I don't think that's right. Our movement, our being, our doing is a pushing against institutionalization.

Do please interrupt me. If you don't I'll carry on, for hours probably.

Q: *John, if I may ...*

J: Yes!

Q: *I'm wondering ... It's fascinating, I have to say your presentation is fascinating and very compelling! It seems to me that there is a spiritual implication to this. I don't want to get you away on a tangent or disrupt the flow and the direction of your comments, but it seems at some level there is a spiritual implication, an implication of spirituality. I'm wondering if you've thought about that or if I'm getting it wrong.*

J: I don't know if you're getting it wrong, but I haven't really thought about it. I don't really think of it in that way. Let's come back to it later.

Q: *Thank you for the concept of We. It is very compassionate and a wonderful idea. In my life, I've always found that to be something I must earn it before I use it, otherwise it's a dangerous illusion that leads to inaction. Whether this is in Selma, Alabama, in '65 or in front of the Pentagon in '67, before we say the word We, we must go inside ourselves and force ourselves to earn that, like the Zapatistas did. Do you have any comments about that?*

J: I wouldn't say earn. I think that We is something that has to be built in practice. We has to be based on some sort of concept of doing. Whether it means going inside ourselves, I don't know. I suppose part of the idea that We are self-contradictory means that changing the world means changing ourselves. And, in that sense, any kind of radical action is also an action against ourselves.

Q: *Yes, I've got a kind of a question. What you're saying sounds good, but it's kind of nebulous. I hate to be a downer, but in any struggle for liberatory social change we ultimately come to the question of force. I mean, what you are saying reminds me of Marx when he was young. He supposedly sarcastically said that demands for liberty, equality, and fraternity would most likely be met by cavalry, infantry, and artillery. And under democratic regimes they're more sophisticated than that. It's not like an old-fashioned historically obsolete monarchical or fascist or Stalinist tyranny. Throughout most advanced capitalist areas of the world you don't see a lot of obvious brutal repression keeping people in line—with the probable exception of the United States—but ultimately . . . I mean, a social movement in the twenty-first century that can abolish the capitalist mode of production and abolish market relations and wage labor and begin the long, difficult process of creating a society worthy of the human beings that live in it, will have to be so large and so self-aware that it can probably curate most necessary social measures and the minimum of violence against other human beings, but not completely. Because* *capitalist social relations are crystallized in certain institutions and in certain harmful individuals and, again, I don't want to be a downer, but those individuals will have to be destroyed. And I'm against Lenin, I'm against Kautsky, and I'm against the Bolsheviks after March 1918, but I'm reminded favorably of lines of Lenin in his letter of advice to the revolutionaries of Hungary in spring 1919. Lenin said to them, among other things, he said, From the beginning, the dictatorship of the proletariat must use swift, implacable, merciless revolutionary violence against exploiters, against capitalists, big landowners, and their supporters, and anyone who does not understand that is not a revolutionary. On that one line, I do agree with Lenin. And, I'm sorry, I don't want to derail what you're saying, because I like it, but there is the downside that has to be addressed too.*

J: Probably the next point I was going to make has to do with that. It's that We don't have the answers. We don't know how to make a revolution. We are confused. To go back to the We, the self-contradictory We. I think if we're going to start talking about—which we are of course, we are talking about radical change and the possibilities of radical change and how to think about radical change—I think that one fundamental aspect of We is that We don't have the answers, We don't know. What we do know is that we have an experience of what revolution meant in the twentieth century. We've seen thousands and millions of people who devoted their lives to trying to create a better society, trying to create a communist society. Thousands and thousands and thousands of people who died for it, who lived for it and then died for it. I think we can now say it didn't work. It didn't work, and in most cases it was worse than not working; it was actually a disaster. I assume that most of us here are committed to the struggle against capitalism, but I would suspect that there are very few people in this room who feel, "Oh, if only I could have lived in the Soviet Union in the 1930s and '40s!" And for it to work we would have to feel that, and we don't, it was actually a disaster. It was a disaster that argu-ably did more than anything else to stabilize capitalism in the twentieth century. I think what happened after the fall of the Soviet Union was that people often became embarrassed about talking about revolution or the need for revolution. Which, of course, is complete nonsense because capitalism becomes worse and worse and worse, more and more destructive. So we have to go back to the question not just of how we have our struggles here and there but how we can actually break the system, how we can break this dynamic of destruction. And we know the answer: the only honest answer is that we don't know. We don't know how to do it. We know that the old idea of revolution failed. We can explain it in different ways in differ-ent countries, of course, we can say, well, Stalin, of course, we can explain China in one way, we can explain Russia in another way, we can explain Cuba—though Cuba is a bit different—in another way, we can explain Albania in a different way. But the point for me is that we also have to draw general lessons. What I would say is that there was something fundamentally wrong with the conception of revolution. There was something fundamentally wrong with the idea that you could bring about the sort of radical change that we want through the state. The reason that it was wrong is because the state is not *our* form of organization. The state is a particular form of organization that excludes, that is hierarchical, that excludes people from the process of social determination. The only way forward is to try and rethink how revolution can be made, how we can think about radical change. And the starting point for rethinking is to say, "Well, We don't actually have all the answers. We don't know what to do."

I don't know. I mean the question of violence, the question of how we confront the use of physical force by the state, is of enormous importance. I don't have any easy answer. I don't have a difficult answer either. I don't have an answer on just how you do it. If we think in terms of organizing ourselves around violence then that fundamentally affects the way we think about social change, the way we think about relations between one another, it has fundamental effects on the way in which we think about the relations between women and men, between young people and old people. To think in terms of armed revolution is really to think in terms of a movement dominated by young men. And that doesn't appeal to me very much.

If we start off by saying, "We don't know," it also takes us—and this is important—into a different sort of politics. Because if we say, "We know how to do it," then, of course, our duty is to explain to the other people how to do it. It takes us into a politics of monologue, of talking to the masses, of explaining to them. Whereas if we start off by saying, "We don't actually know; We're full of ideas and experiences, but We don't have the answers," then that immediately takes us into a politics of dialogue, where we are saying, "I don't know, what do you think? How do you think we can do it?" One of the basic principles of the Zapatistas is this idea of politics in terms of "Asking, We Walk." The way we move forward is by asking, by drawing people into discussion. Asking them, getting them involved in an active discussion, an active process of listening and talking. And that, I think, is very important. I know you want to come back to . . . Let me just go on and then we'll come back to it.

So we're confused. Also, we're in crisis. One thing I've been thinking recently is that it's easy to say well, we know that the revolutions of the twentieth century have failed and we know that state-centered politics doesn't seem to work very well; it doesn't seem to bring about the fundamental changes that we want. Therefore, we have to think of a different kind of politics. But I think that we also have to be aware that the current struggles in places like Greece and Spain also confront us with our own crisis. In Greece you've got, on the one hand, this appalling politics of austerity and, on the other hand, you have the most militant tradition of struggle, both state-centered struggle and anarchist struggle and autonomous creative struggle, certainly in Europe, and one of the most important traditions in the world, and they've been struggling and struggling and struggling and doing everything possible. But they haven't actually succeeded in breaking the dynamic of austerity. I think we have to see that that's our crisis too, it confronts us with the limits of our own thinking.

I think that's where we are. I could go on, I'm not going to go on. Let's talk. I know you wanted to come back, there was somebody there who wanted to go back to . . .

Q: *I just have two comments. One is the eventual idea of communism and socialism, what I understand, was to do—they called it—the "withering away of the state." So they had this idea that the state was, in the long run, a bad actor, but maybe their error was seeing the transition through state power and then they got stuck there. The other thing is the state provides many services to people, things like health care, in some states more than they do in this country, and in many of the very conservative—which I think in some ways many of us have something in common with, though we don't like to think that—they're nervous about the state as well, maybe for different reasons. There are people who think that all good things come from the state, but in a transitional period there are services and ways of living that really have to be centralized. So, I just wanted you to comment on that kind of different way of looking at any kind of transition.*

J: Shall we take interventions three by three?

Q: *Yeah, I just wanted to respond to that, about all these services. That somehow, miraculously, when the state sets up those services, it does it in the most reactionary, demeaning way. So I think that point . . . somehow, I have no idea how, autonomous organizations and movements somehow supply them not going through the organs of the state.*

Q: *I want to know what an institution is and what you understand by anti-institutional. When does an organization become an institution?*

J: Well, on the first two, which really go together, I suppose basically I agree with the second, with what you were saying. It does seem to me it's a very complicated thing. If we think of health care, if we think of education, if we think of social services to help the poor . . . I spent a lot of my life in Britain. In that sense I grew up with the idea of the National Health Service and it does seem to me that that is so important, the idea that you can go to a doctor and you don't have to think at all about money and you can go to hospital and you don't have to think at all about money. So I appreciate that. On the other hand, if you think of what health means, of what education means, of what aid to the poor means when administered by the state, then it is clear that it imposes certain concepts of health and well-being, certain concepts of education, certain concepts of mutual aid, I suppose (which is not mutual aid; it is state-administered aid), which I think run counter to the sort of society that we would want to create. But, on the other hand, I think precisely, as the comrade there said, we do have to think actively about how we build other ways of dealing with these issues. Again, if you look—I keep on citing the Zapatistas, I don't really want to, it's just they come to mind all the time—there they've been building up over the last twenty years their own system of education, of organization, of mutual support, of justice, of how you deal with criminals, etc., which are very much embedded within the community and come from them. And that is, for me, part of the process of revolution that we have to think of.

On the question of the withering away of the state, which I think was Engels in particular, I suppose I feel he got it wrong. He got it wrong in the sense that I don't think that we can do things that way. If you think of the state as a specific form of social organization, the state is a way of doing things, a way of relating to people, a way of doing things that actually excludes people. State education, in a sense, excludes the children. State medicine excludes the patients from the process. If you think of the state as a way of doing things then you can say, "Well no, because what we want is actually to create a different society, in which things are done in different ways and that is the only way we can build our strength."

The third question, on institutions and what is an institution. I suppose what I think of as an institution is an established or habitual way of doing things. We institutionalize a practice, supposing we say here, this evening, we're all going to come back tomorrow, and we'll all come back the day after and next week again at the same time, and Tuesday, Wednesday, Thursday, and the week after that, Tuesday, Wednesday, Thursday, then this may be an appealing practice, it may be fine, but what I feel is that it gradually gets hollowed out, it gradually becomes a set of rules that loses its own force. If you think of assemblies, again, I think they can become institutionalized, but if an assembly is to have life, it has to be something that people come to because they are enthusiastic about it and when they're not, they'll stay away from it. In other words, any kind of establishment of patterns is always an attempt to lay down what people in the future will do. I think that that is generally harmful; not always, but on the whole it is not the way to think about the sort of change that we want to create.

On the other hand, I do feel that in some ways, because of our own limitations, we need institutions. Here, we are in an institution, aren't we, in the CIIS, the After Capitalism program. I work in an institution as well in Puebla, which I like very much indeed. I think that we do have a tendency to fall into institutions, but we have to constantly move beyond them, we have to think beyond them, we have to think of moving on.

Q: *Thank you so much for coming to talk to us. I'm really enjoying your honest reflections and I think this is very important. Going* back to the question of institutions and maybe connected to the question of transition. My concern with these discussions at the moment and thinking about creating autonomous organizations and whatnot, which basically I agree with, but I'm also concerned about transition being the same exact motto of neoliberalism. The whole idea of the destruction of public education and also of faith-based initiatives, etc., and the idea that we want to flush the state down the drain because the government is not the solution, it's the problem. And my question here is, of course, we all do know that, is how do we confront this issue which way back the Greeks were already confronting with the [inaudible] freedom and necessity. But you just said, a moment, structure and antistructure, so how can we proceed? Because if we lose some of the elements, as bad as the state may be, in some states there was an accumulation of social knowledge and wealth and possibility which will be destroyed completely with going back to field times [inaudible] and to the lords and the ladies and so to the lady Thatcher [inaudible].

Q: I wanted to go back to the question of the We, which I think is such an important pronoun in our time, because I've been seeing a lot of the invocation of the We in the climate crisis currently and I think it is being invoked by scientists with the best of intentions in a very undifferentiated way. Scientists say we are in trouble, we are destroying the planet, but I think it needs to be stated that some of us are destroying the planet more than others, some vicious states, some corporations, so the problem is how to differentiate the We. How to break up that We. It captures the imagination because we want to. Our best aspiration is to think of the We as the species, or even beyond the species, as living beings or any kind of being on the planet. And so the problem of the We is always who is outside of the We. In this case, environmentally, I feel it needs to be stated that those who are advocating climate adaptation of spaceship earth, which is really fortress Europe, fortress U.S., that's not the We that I want to subscribe to, any *more than universal humanity, under the regime of empire, was a humanity that was inclusive. So, I'm just wondering how you think of the We that you want to invoke in the context of this We of the scientists and environmentalists and of climate adapters.*

Q: *I'd like to ask about dialogue. It's very critical, very important. Can you give us some advice on your experiences on how you have accomplished meaningful dialogue with people like Zapatistas and others. It would be very helpful, I think. Thank you.*

J: On the first question about neoliberalism, which really goes back to one of your questions which I haven't answered properly about what about the right wing, the ultraconservative attacks on the state. They really go together. And Mrs. Thatcher. If we think of the bits of the state that we don't perhaps hate as much as other bits of the state, then I think we have to say yes . . . Once again, I will relate back to my British experience of the welfare state, including the National Health Service, the education system, the fact that, at least when I was a student, of course you didn't pay in the universities and of course you received a grant to go to universities and everybody did, everybody who got into the universities. And fantastic! You can say that a lot of the twentieth century was dominated, I suppose, by the push to drive back the rule of money, to struggle against the rule of the commodity, to push against the commodification of absolutely everything. And you can think of the revolutions in Russia and China and the other places as attempts to break commodification, to push back the rule of money. Tremendously important. You can think also the whole social democratic movement as part of the drive to push back the rule of money. Yes, great, people fought and fought and fought for these changes and they have to be respected. But then you can say, well yes, but of course what happened to those struggles is that they were re-formed by the state. They were given a different form. The struggles were expropriated from the people who were struggling. The state education that came out wasn't an education dominated by the people. And you can understand the reaction of people against that as well. The experience of state education in many cases is a very unpleasant experience. If we think of our richness in terms of the richness of our creativeness, that was the point about the quotation from the *Grundrisse* at the beginning, if you think of that, then no, education doesn't allow that kind of richness to expand and develop.

If these Zapatista responses to real social struggles are attacked, as they are attacked by neoliberalism, what do we do? I think what we do is say, "No, we have to fight for the decommodification of education; we have to push back the rule of money." We have to start from where that push against the rule of money got to and say, "Yes, but we have to take it further, and we have to drive it further and further." Oh, just a footnote about what you were saying about the Right! One thing that seems to me that we have to do and we don't—at least I haven't seen this seriously discussed—is we worry about rethinking the Left, but we're not really rethinking the whole concept of the Right, and what we mean by the Right. I think we need to. We need to see that, in the same way in which the Left is contradictory, we need as well to rethink the concept of the Right. I don't know what the implications of that are, it just seems to me important. What I would say is the core of the problem with state institutions takes us to Eddie's very difficult question about the We.

What I said a moment ago is that the We is self-contradictory because We exist in and against the current society. I also talked about our richness and our dignity. In a way, what I was trying to say is that the basis on which all of these are founded is actually our creative power. Our power to do, our power to create. If we think of it, the basis of capitalism is that it takes our doing, our creative power and it abstracts it. It draws it into a form of social cohesion that we do not control. It takes our richness, the richness of our creative capacities and, through the operation of money or through the commodity, it pulls it into the system, so that our creative abilities, our richness, are being dragged into a form that we don't control. If you think of the basis of what We are, if we think of ourselves not as human *beings* but as human *doers*—in other words what makes us human is our doing, is our activity, is our ability to think about our activity, to project our activity, to work cooperatively—if you think of that then the loss of that ability to control our own doing is the fundamental criticism of capitalism. If we start off by thinking of dignity, if we start off thinking about richness, we're thinking of capitalism as a system of frustration. Before exploitation, the problem of capitalism is that it frustrates us, it doesn't allow us to develop our richness, it doesn't allow us to develop our doing, our creative capacity. Our creative capacity is drawn into this system, but not entirely. Because if we were entirely drawn in, then we wouldn't be able to talk about it. And Marx talks about that right at the beginning of *Capital*. He says that the key to understand everything about capitalism is the dual nature of labor. The antagonism, if you like, between our concrete labor, our ability to do things, our ability to create our own projects or worlds, and abstract or alienated labor, the labor that we are drawn into, where that creative capacity is taken away from us. By starting off by talking about dignity, by talking about We, by talking about richness, we are saying yes, but not entirely! Our creative ability is not entirely lost within the capitalistic system, we overflow from that. We go beyond, we exist beyond that, and that is precisely what we are trying to do here: we are trying to create something that doesn't follow the logic of capital. That's what you're trying to do in CIIS. That is what we're trying to do in so many projects, in so many creative things here and all over the world. We're actually moving beyond, trying to create something that doesn't fit in.

To go on to Eddie's question about the We, the We is a We that says We are dispossessed and We will take the world that is ours. That's the great thing about the Occupy movement, it's not just that they're putting up tents in squares here and there; they're saying We are occupying the world because the world is ours and how dare they take it away from us. That's the point about starting with We and dignity and richness, it's that we're starting with this idea that the world is ours, it is ours to create. And if you pose We in those terms, then I think you're saying that We is the foundation, We is creating a self-determining process of doing, of creativity, which goes against money, which is the negation of our possibility of self-creation. And there is your distinguishing line. We don't have to say they're the baddies, we're the goodies, because once you get into that it seems to me disastrous. No, we have to say We means a way of doing. They don't have that way of doing. If they want to give up being chief executives or whatever and come and join us in building a community garden, fine! It's not necessarily that we hate them as individuals, what we hate is their way of organizing things, their way of subjecting our activity to a certain logic, to a logic of destruction. That's very important, as well, if we think back to the dictatorship of the proletariat and Pannekoek, who criticized Lenin for his concept of the dictatorship of the proletariat. He said, well, the problem with Lenin is that he thinks of the dictatorship of the proletariat in personal terms. So that those people who are not proletariat have to be eliminated. Pannekoek says that No, it's not about that, it's about the way that we organize, and that if we organize on the basis of factory councils, then we find that the capitalists don't come along; they're going to be eliminated from that process. If we think of organization in terms of assemblies, then that itself is a process of exclusion. That itself is the way in which the We takes shape.

So, really, the basis of it all, the basis of dignity, the basis of richness, the basis of self-contradiction, the basis of everything else I said is to understand ourselves as the movement of doing against labor. The movement of the doing that comes from us. We do what we think is desirable or necessary or enjoyable. But not because of the logic that is imposed upon us by money and by profit. So that We is really the movement of doing against labor. If you think of all these projects and movements, if you think of tonight, if you think of the CIIS, if you think of what we're trying to do in Puebla, if you think of the Zapatistas, if you think of the uprisings all over the place, then this is precisely it, it is people saying We will shape what We think is right. We will not shape our lives according to the logic of money. That, for me, is the composition of the We. I suppose that is your "earning" as well, isn't it? What you were saying earlier on about "we need to earn it," or we need to create the We through the processes of cooperation. To go against the logic of money, to try and recapture or reoccupy doing. I don't want it to sound abstract. I suppose the danger of all that I've been saying is that it may sound abstract, but in fact it's not! It's what the movements are saying; it's what is happening. If you look at the anticapitalist movements over the last twenty, thirty years, they've been developing new concepts, they've been developing the We. What they've been developing, above all, is this idea that we can't just think of exploitation, we can't just think of our struggle against capitalism as being a struggle against exploitation. Of course that's part of it; exploitation is inherent in abstract labor, which is the basis of a whole system of social cohesion, a whole system that pulls us all together in a way that destroys us, in a way that destroys us personally and destroys our possibilities of creation and is destroying us as a society. The problem is not just exploitation. It's not just a question of working class against capitalist class. The problem is how we break this system of social cohesion and the system of social cohesion is established through money. And behind money lies abstract labor: the deadly social cohesion is established through the abstraction of doing into labor. I think that that is what is happening, that that is where the We arises from, and why people are often reluctant to talk about the working class. If we think of our movement as the movement of doing against labor, then we have to say our movement is the movement of doers who are forced to labor against that labor. So, it is a working-class movement against work in the sense of alienated labor and against being classified. That is what the struggle of the working class is about. Once you say the secret is not about taking power, the challenge is how we uncouple ourselves, how we break away from the system of social cohesion. Even within the existing society, how do we develop forms of doing things that push in the other direction, that make sense and that can be possible embryos of a future society?

I think that's what happening. I don't know whether you're all into reading *Capital*—you should be, you must be. The movement is leading to a reinterpretation of *Capital*, where people are beginning to move from the chapters on exploitation and focus more on the question of value and the way in which capitalism should be seen, in the first place, as a system of social cohesion. A system of social cohesion which at the same time is not a system of social cohesion, because the only way we can talk about it as a system of social cohesion is if we ourselves are bursting out of it, if we ourselves are bursting beyond it. And that's what dignity is about, it's about saying we won't follow the rules of the game. It's about saying We will create, our dignity means that We are creators, our dignity means that We are doers, our dignity means that We will not just follow the logic of the system, We will create other things. We will create other spaces, we will create other times. So I think that's how we have to think about the We.

Of course, you are completely right, the We can be used in very loose ways, but somehow we have to pin it down and say that We means the social self-determination of our own doing, of our own creativity. And that's what people are already saying.

The other question was about meaningful dialogue. I think that's part of the same thing, I think that meaningful dialogue is this process of liberating our doing and part of that is liberating our talking.

Andrej: It's already nine o'clock, so we have to end for tonight, but John is going to be back tomorrow and the day after tomorrow. The topic for tomorrow is social cohesiveness of capital, something that strangles us, right? And, finally, the last topic which is going to be on Thursday is . . .

J: We Are the Crisis of Capital.

A: Sounds beautiful!

TWO

Capital, the Social Cohesion That Strangles Us

For those of you who weren't here last night or for those of you who may not remember, let me start off by telling you the story so far.

We started at the beginning, and what better starting place than to start with ourselves? We started with We. What we want to finish up with, but not today, what we want to finish up with tomorrow, is that We Are the Crisis of Capital. And proud of it.

We started at the beginning, and what better starting place than to start with ourselves? The starting point is important because if we start with domination, if we start with structures, then there is a great danger that we enclose ourselves, that we entrap ourselves within the structures of domination that we want to criticize. Once we create a framework of domination for ourselves, for our own thought, our own argument, really there is no way out. It's important, I think, to start with the force that can break those structures. It's important to start with something that is not closure, with something that is openness, with breaking. In other words, it is important to start with ourselves.

I made various points about We very briefly.

First, We are dignity, We are not victims. We are dignity and We are dignified rage. We are *digna rabia*, as the Zapatistas put it.

Second, We are richness. We are the rich, not the poor. It is not because we are poor that we rebel, it is because we are rich, because we have in us the enormous richness of undefined creativity. And it is because this richness and this dignity is incarcerated within the forms of capital, within the commodity form, that we rise up and say no, we will not accept it. We don't start from the poor, we start from the rich. We don't start from being victims, we start from our own dignity. We are dignity, We are richness, We are the only creators of this society, and therefore we are the creators upon whom capital depends. We are in rebellion, otherwise I don't know why you would be here this evening if you weren't, in some sense, in rebellion. We are in rebellion not because We are special; our rebellion doesn't make us different from all those masses who didn't come this evening. We are in rebellion because We are ordinary. That is the greatest challenge of the Zapatistas, they say, "We are perfectly ordinary people, therefore we are rebels." We are ordinary dignities and our politics is the politics of trying to articulate and recognize the dignities of all of us. And that leads us to certain ideas about political organization. It leads us to considering ourselves part of the great anticapitalist tradition that goes back to the very origins of anticapitalism, that understands organization in terms of assemblies, in terms of councils, in terms of soviets, in terms of communes, in terms of organizing in a way that tries to articulate our anger and doesn't think about organization from an instrumental point of view, as simply how to gain power.

We are self-contradictory. And We are confused. We are self-contradictory because we must be, because our feet are caught in the mud of the society in which we live, even if our heads want to break away from it. Or perhaps it's the other way round, perhaps it's our heads that are caught in the mud of the society in which we live and our feet want to get away from it or are already running. But, in any case, the contradictions of this society are bound to reproduce themselves within us. So, inevitably, living in an antagonistic society means that we, too, are self-antagonistic. And that means that the concept or the very idea of revolutionary purity is a load of nonsense. It is not just a load of nonsense, it is absolutely destructive. That also leads us to the idea that the only way forward is not by laying down the correct line but, again as the Zapatistas put it, asking. Asking, we walk. We advance by asking, by trying to connect with the other dignities that surround us, the other rebellions that surround us. We try and move forward through discussion, through hearing, through asking people about their rebelliousness, about their dignity.

We misfit. We misfit into this society. We misfit not because, or not only because, we are weird people on the edges of society, but we misfit because misfitting is actually a central aspect of existence in a capitalist society, because capital is the pushing of human lives into forms within which we cannot possibly fit. Capital pushes our activity into the labor form. It pushes our relations with one another into the commodity form or into the money form. And it can't work! It can have a huge effect, it obviously does, a huge, disastrous, destructive effect. But it's not totally successful, it can't be totally successful. And if it were totally successful we wouldn't have any way of talking about it. So we misfit.

We exist. The very fact of existing within capitalist society means we exist in, against, and beyond capitalist society. We exist in capitalism, and that has a huge effect on the way we think and what we do. But we also inevitably exist against capitalist society, because the very fact of being forced to exist in it forces us to protest against it, to rebel against it, to reject it. We exist in and against it, but also beyond capitalist society, because all the time we are trying to create something else, to create forms of relating to other people that are more adequate to what we are or what we think we are, or what we think we could be. So all the time we are not only in but also against, and we are also pushing beyond society, which means we don't fit in. We don't fit into any boxes, and we don't fit into any identities. So our politics, our anti-capitalism, is inevitably an anti-identitarian politics. An anti-identitarian politics which says, "Fine, OK, we are women or we are gay or we are black or we are Irish or we are indigenous, but we are more than that." And if we don't say that, if we don't recognize how we spill over from our own identities, then it does seem to me that our language becomes too easily integrated, it becomes, I would say, reactionary. And, although it is the fifth time I refer to them and I don't know if I should go on talking about them, what seems to me to be exciting about the Zapatistas is not just that it is an indigenous movement. If they were just an indigenous movement we would say, "Oh great, very good, we'll show you our solidarity, good you're doing that, fine." But no, it's not that. They have said from the beginning, "We are a movement which is almost totally indigenous in composition, but we are not just an indigenous movement. We are not just fighting for indigenous rights, we are actually fighting for humanity." From the beginning, it is a movement that spills over. It consciously spills over from its own identity and that's what makes them exciting.

We overflow, then. We overflow from our identities, and I think that means also that We are anti-institutional. If We exist in, against, and beyond, then it means that We are in movement, it means that We are not nouns, We are actually verbs. We are movings, We are doings, We are human doings, We are verbs. And that means, I think, that We are anti-institutional. Institutions try to convert our verbness into nouns. They try to fix it, give it stability. They try to tie down our potentially unlimited becoming.

And finally, We are doers against labor. We are not just labor; we are actually doers against labor. If we think of the way in which capital entraps our dignity or imprisons our dignity, if we think of the way in which the commodity form or the money form incarcerates our richness, the richness of our potential, then we can say that the basis of that is actually that capital incarcerates our doing, our activity, and forces it into the form of a labor that produces value or contributes to the production of value and therefore contributes to the production of capitalist profit. To say We are against capital, we absolutely have to say that We are against labor, in the sense that we are against capitalist labor, we are against what capital does to our activity as humans. And I think that is something that is actually becoming articulated more and more in anticapitalist movements over the last fifteen to twenty years or thirty years: the idea that no, we cannot think of anticapitalism simply as being the struggle of labor against capital. It is, in the first place, and must be, the struggle of doing against labor. Against the labor that produces capital. Which doesn't mean, and perhaps I should emphasize that, it doesn't mean that our struggle is therefore outside the factory. In a way, on the contrary. Well, not on the contrary exactly, but partly on the contrary, because if we think of the people who suffer most directly from the imposition of labor upon doing, if you think of the people who suffer most directly, most painfully, from the subjection of their activity to the demands of labor that produces value or contributes to the production of value, then of course that means people who are employed, including obviously people who are in the factories. So, to say that our movement is the movement of doing against labor is not at all to say that our movement is outside the factories, but that our movement, whether within or without or wherever, is a movement of doing against labor, a movement for the recuperation of the self-determination of our own activity as humans. And that's really what it's all about, isn't it? And all this, all these points about We, can be seen not just in terms of abstract ideas of a professor; they are actually points that are emerging from the changing forms of social struggle, of anticapitalist struggle, over the last twenty years or so.

So that's the story so far, that's where we got to last night.

For me, what these three evenings are about is trying to think through or trying to talk about a change that is taking place in the concept of revolution. A change that is taking place in the way we understand anticapitalist struggle. And that has to be a discussion, because our ideas, and I think the ideas of everybody, are in the process of formation. What we can say, I think, is that the collapse of the Soviet Union and the emergence of China as an aggressive capitalist power have made very clear, I think almost to everybody, what had already been said for many years before that. Namely, that the revolutions in China, in Russia, were a failure. Or that there was something wrong with the whole idea of revolution in the twentieth century. They can all be explained, of course, in terms of particular historical events, but there was something wrong in the way that people were talking about revolution. And, of course, thousands and thousands and millions of people fought and devoted their lives to those ideas of revolution and they devoted their lives to trying to make the world a different place, they devoted their lives and their deaths to a struggle to get rid of capitalism. Obviously, I think we are their heirs. We have to take that very seriously, it places a responsibility on us. That responsibility is not to say, "Ugh, they were filthy Stalinists or Trotskyists" or whatever; the responsibility on us is really to pick up the banners that they have left fallen on the ground. The only way that we can pick up those banners, I think, is by going off in a slightly different direction. The only way we can honor their memory is by saying, "Wow, fantastic, wonderful how you fought for a different society, but you were wrong. You were fantastic, but the way you thought about bringing about change was mistaken. We have learned, we have learned from your experience in the last century that that doesn't work. And so, to honor your memory, we have to take up the question of revolution again, but the only way we can take up the question of revolution is by rethinking what it means, by trying to reset the terms." What happened after the fall of the Soviet Union and China was that there was an initial reaction that said, "Well, revolution isn't really on the cards, and there's not much point in talking about revolution or thinking about revolution anymore, but of course struggles are important." And that's not necessarily bad because, I think, perhaps what happened is that people, instead of wasting their energies on building up the party or on fighting out sectarian disputes with other parties—of course that continued and continues—but I think that perhaps people started to put more energy into actually fighting local struggles or fighting for particular things, struggles that set out to change and improve the world and, in some cases, have done so. But in that process, very often, the whole question of revolution became lost. Now I think we have to go back to the idea of revolution, because it's not just a question of winning little victories here and there, which we sometimes do but generally don't, but it's not that. It's a question of how on earth do we break the dynamic of existing society, how on earth do we break the dynamic of capital, the dynamic of money that is causing such appalling destruction throughout the world, appalling destruction to our lives, appalling destruction to other forms of life, appalling destruction to everything.

How on earth do we break that dynamic? How do we go beyond or how do we understand the particular struggles in the context of a possible dynamic, or a dynamic that seeks to break, or a push that seeks to break the dynamic of destruction? All these individual struggles are great, but I think we need to go back to the question of what revolution means today. How can we think, not just from a professorial point of view or from the point of view of a PhD or whatever, but how can we think on the basis of the development of struggles, how can we see a different conception of revolution being opened up? And for me that takes us back, in the first place, to what I was saying yesterday about We, and We are dignity and We are richness and We are self-contradictory and We are confused and all the rest of it. Because when we start with We, the point is that we are starting with the force or forces of rupture. If we want to talk about how We are going to break the dynamic, then we have to talk about the forces or the force that can break that dynamic. I think it's no good to just say, "Well, the working class will break the dynamic of capital," because that really doesn't help us to think anew. It doesn't help us to open up new questions or try and think about new ways of posing the problems. I'm quite happy to say that the working class is the only force that can break the dynamic of capital, but only if we question the meaning of working class, only if we say we have to understand the working class as the movement of doing against labor. In other words, only if we understand working class as a movement against its own existence as working class. Then yes, perhaps.

When we were talking about We, we were talking about the forces of rupture. We're talking about the force of doing against labor. We're talking about understanding our richness, our dignity, our creativity, our doing, as being the forces of production. Rethinking the whole category of the forces of production, rethinking this whole conflict which is so embedded in the Marxist tradition, rethinking the conflict between the forces of production and the relations of production and saying, "Well, of course, We are the forces of production. Who else is going to create? It has to be We!" We, not just here and now, but We and our fathers and our grandfathers and our great-grandmothers and our great-great-grandmothers etc., in other words that We are part of a continuous development of human creativity. That's surely what the forces of production is all about. We will come back to this later.

So, in talking about We as the force of rupture, how is it that we can understand ourselves as the force that ruptures or that can rupture this terrible dynamic of destruction? One obvious thing to say is, "Well, We are, of course We are, we know We are, but our ruptures are like volcanic ruptures. They are sporadic ruptures, they are occasional ruptures, and they are ruptures that don't exist in the same intensity in all places and at all times. If we look around us, if we just look at the people in this room, then I'm quite sure that we can see how our force is the force of breaking here and there, is the force of cracking the texture of capitalist domination. All of us, in one way or another, break through the dynamic, the cohesive logic of capital by saying, "No, sorry, we're not going to do things that way; we're going to do something else, we're going to walk in the opposite direction." You can think of these as being cracks in this closely woven weave of domination within which we live.

What are those cracks? We can see some cracks easily enough, we can see—that's the sixth or seventh time tonight—we can see the Zapatistas, If you go into the Zapatista areas in Chiapas, you pass a sign that says "Bad Government Stay Out, Here the People Rule." This is obviously a declaration that here, in this territory, We are walking in the opposite direction. We're not going to let the government in and We are not going to follow the logic of the government. We are not going to follow the logic of capital. We are going to organize ourselves in a different way. We are going to create an education that is different and pushes in another direction. We are going to organize a system of health care that pushes in a different direction, a system of justice that doesn't slot into the categories of capital. Obviously, there is a crack. A fantastic, lovely crack that's been going on for twenty years or more. And then you think, "Well, yes, but they're Mexicans. They're far away." And then you think, "Well, what about Occupy Oakland?" for example, to come closer to home. I was being told all about Occupy Oakland about half an hour ago. Wasn't that a crack, wasn't that a space where people were saying not only No, not only protesting but actually trying to create something different, actually trying to walk in the other direction, actually trying to create different sorts of social relations, actually trying to work out in practice the basis for some new form or different form of social organization? So there you've got a medium-sized crack, that hasn't lasted perhaps for the twenty years that the Zapatistas have existed publicly, but of course it's an important crack. And then you think well, OK, what about us? What about us here, tonight, what are we doing, what are we talking about? We're not talking about how we can make a profit on our next essay or on our next dissertation or whatever, we're not talking about how we slot into the system. We're talking about how we can go in the opposite direction. How we can think in the opposite direction, how we can think against capital, how we can give a force to our own thought against capital, our own rejection of capital. You think well yes, that's nice, even if we're only going to last three days, perhaps, or a few hours, here we've got a crack too, we're trying to push in the opposite direction. It's not because we have some ambition to advance within the system of education, it's because this is actually what has meaning for us. This is actually what is important to us. And then you begin to look around and to think, well yes, there are lots, you can think of big cracks, you can think of the Zapatistas, you can think of Oaxaca, you can think of Buenos Aires in 2001–2002, you can think of . . . oh, 1968, there's a lovely big crack! You can think on and on and on. Or you can think of small or medium cracks or little cracks, you can think of autonomous radio stations, you can think of alternative education experiments, you can think of community gardens, you can think of all sort of things that go in the wrong direction. Then you begin to think, well yes, sometimes these cracks are territorial, sometimes they mark out a clear territorial space. They say here is a Zapatista area, or here Oaxaca, or here Zuccotti Park or whatever. Here we've got a little space.

But you don't have to think of it in territorial terms, you can think of it in terms of time. You can say, well, OK, we live in a society in which there are all sorts of pressures that push us to conform, but even in that context we can say No. There are times in which we will express our fury, times in which we will express our search for something else. Here we are, meeting for a couple of hours. This is a temporally defined crack I suppose. But one that we hope spills over and over and over and over. Or you can think of it as being activity-related. You can say we live in a capitalist society. We live, at least for the moment, unfortunately, in a society in which products are sold as commodities. But water, no. No way will we accept the commodification of water. And then you rise up like the people in Cochabamba in the year 2000 in the war of water and say, "No, we will not accept the privatization of water." And they won. Or you rise up like the students of the UNAM, the main university of Mexico City, again in 1999–2000, and say, "No, we will not accept the introduction of fees, because that is the first step towards the privatization of public education." And they fought and they fought and they went on strike for ten months! And in the end they were repressed. But they won on that point. And since then no rector has even dared to mention the possibility of introducing fees. So you begin to look around, you begin to see that in fact we were right to start with We, we were right to start with overflowing, we were right not to start with domination, because when you look at the world you actually see that the world is full of cracks, full of these spaces of rejection, of refusal and creation, in which people push in the opposite direction.

One thing that characterizes all these cracks is that in those spaces, in those moments, in those activities, people are saying here, in this space, in this moment, in relation to this, we reject the integration of our activity into capitalism. We reject the logic of alienated labor, we reject the logic of abstract labor, we reject the logic of value, we reject the logic of money. Here we shall do what we consider to be desirable, what we consider to be necessary. So the core of these cracks is actually a revolt of doing against labor. This is something we are all aware of, and all these things have been developing and growing, they've been there all the time, but I think they've been developing with a new confidence over the last twenty, thirty years. We have all sorts of names for them. We talk about them as autonomies, as autonomous spaces. We can talk about them as dignities; here we raise the flag of dignity and go in the opposite direction. We can think of them as being no-go areas, areas in which we will not allow capital to dominate, in which we will not allow money to dominate. We do it all the time, we do it also in our personal life. In a sense, that is what we mean by love. If we love somebody, if we love our children, if we love our partner or whoever, we are saying, "Here it's a different logic. We are not going to relate to our children or our loved ones on the basis of money. We are not going to try and think how will we get a good price for our children." That is part of the pushing in the opposite direction which is profoundly rooted in our everyday experience. Or you can talk of them, as Chris Carlsson does, as nowtopias, or you can talk of them, as Rebecca Solnit does, as paradises, a concept that is associated with the whole history of gardening. The way we fight is not, or not just, by looking for gradual reform, but it is by lifting an area of experience or a territorial area, lifting an area out of capital and, within that area, creating something else. In a way, you can think of it as us raising so many banners of a different world, or creating so many lighthouses that illuminate and shine onto the world and inspire people.

The reason why I like talking about cracks rather than autonomies is because, for me, cracks suggest movement. Cracks move all the time. They expand, they get covered over, they get plastered over, they open again, they join up, they are in constant movement. Whereas the danger, for me, of thinking in terms of an autonomous space or the danger in the practice of autonomous spaces is that they can become closed in on themselves. Once they cease to move then they cease to break, they cease to be ruptures. So that's why I talk about cracks, but you don't have to, call them what you like.

If that corresponds to what had been happening in anti-capitalist struggle over recent years, we can say that this is the basis of a different way of thinking about revolution. We can begin to say, "Well, if we're going to pose the question of revolution again, we have to pose it not in terms of how we're going to take state power; that didn't work. We now have to think of revolution in terms of the creation, expansion, multiplication, and confluence of these cracks." Another way of saying that is that we have to think of revolution as being interstitial. We can't think of revolution as being the complete transformation of the whole world from one day to another. We have to think in terms of an interstitial process, a process of multiple ruptures. We have to think that capital won't be killed by a dagger-thrust to the heart; it will actually be killed by millions and millions of bee stings. And we are the bees that are stinging it and are going to keep on stinging it until it dies.

But if you say revolution has to be interstitial, in a sense that has always been true. The whole notion of taking state power was also an interstitial concept of revolution. You take control of one state, and then another state and another state— that is very clear, for example, in the Trotskyist idea of permanent revolution and the rejection of the idea of socialism in one country. Of course revolution has to be interstitial. But what is emerging now is the awareness that we have to think of these interstices, or these spaces, or these cracks, autonomies, as being *our* spaces. It doesn't work if we pour our rebellion into the organizational forms created for the reproduction of capital. Because to pour our rebellions into the state form, into capitalist forms, means to expropriate ourselves, means to exclude ourselves from our own rebellion. I was in Bolivia about five or six years ago and I had this feeling after the election of Evo Morales, and the MAS government, after the whole upsurge of rebellion from 2000 to 2005. What was happening was exciting, but it was a revolution expropriated. It was a process that had actually been taken away from the people who were creating it, or who had created the basis for it. And I think that has become ever more clear since then.

So, not through the state. If we are talking about cracks we are saying No, the cracks have to be *our* cracks, *our* forms of organization, *our* rethinkings of social relations. If we say No to the state, and this is surely fundamental, then we shoot clocks. This is the lovely thing of Walter Benjamin, in his "Theses on the Philosophy of History," where he says that in 1830, the first thing that the workers did in the uprising in Paris was they went out and shot the clocks. They took out their guns and fired at the clocks in the towers. In other words, if we say not through the state, then we have to rethink time. Because the state implies a certain concept of time, if we think of revolution as taking place through the state, then inevitably we think of the revolution as being in the future. We think of the Future Revolution. And we build for the glorious day, we build a party, we build the organization, we perhaps build the army or whatever, but we are building for the future, when we will take power and then we will bring about change. What is happening at the moment is exactly the opposite. The idea of creating cracks means creating revolution here and now. We won't wait, we can't wait. The idea of "Oh, there might be a socialist revolution in fifty years' time or in a hundred years' time. Well, of course we won't live to see it but perhaps our children or our grandchildren will," that idea is absolutely insane! It's insane because who knows if humans will still exist in a hundred years' time for a start off, if we don't do something to change the system. It's ridiculous! In other words, we have to think of the revolution as being here and now. And that's exactly what the cracks are doing. They are saying, "Here, in our little area perhaps we're mad, perhaps we're insignificant, but here and now we are going to transform things. Here and now we are going to do things in a different way." That doesn't solve the problem but it changes the temporalities. In the old traditional idea of revolution there are two temporalities. The first temporality is wait. Revolutionary patience. They have always talked about the virtue of revolutionary patience. Wait until the conditions are right, until we build our organization strong enough. This year in the election we managed to get one percent of the vote, next year it's going to be two percent and maybe in ten years time we'll be up to four percent, so just a bit of revolutionary patience and we will get there in the end. So, the first temporality is the temporality of patience and then, of course, when the great day comes, then complete transformation.

I think that now, with the cracks, we have a reversal of temporalities. Again we have two temporalities. The first temporality is here and now we change things, we change things because we cannot stand it, we cannot accept what is happening. ¡Ya Basta! Here and now, enough! And we start walking in the wrong direction, here and now we start doing things in a different way. But I think there is also a second temporality, because we know all too well that the fact that we start to walk in the different direction does not unfortunately mean that capitalism will no longer exist tomorrow. It may do, I'm not saying it necessarily will exist tomorrow, but at least we know that it doesn't necessarily mean that just because we walk in the wrong direction then capitalism will disappear. In other words, the Zapatista "¡Ya Basta!" is complemented by another expression of theirs, which is "We walk, we do not run, because we are going a long way." In other words, there is behind the impatience, the refusal to say accept anymore, there is an arduous process of actually creating a different world.

So, if we ask not just what clever ideas can we find about revolution today but what is it that the struggles themselves are saying about revolution, then I think what they are doing is that they are posing the issue of revolution not in terms of taking power, not in terms of party politics and winning elections; they are posing the issue of revolution in terms of how do we break the logic of capital, how can we create spaces that go in the opposite direction, how can we break the social cohesion that lies so heavily upon us? How can we break the social syn-thesis within which we live, how can we break this totality that sucks us all in so awfully, so unbearably, so horribly all the time? We rebel, We want to do something different, and all the time there's this horrible sucking noise that pulls us back into the logic of the system. How can we break that and how do we think about revolution? I think now this is the issue, not as the replacement of one totality by another totality, which was the old idea: you break capitalism and create a different total social system; you get rid of capitalism and install socialist planning which is going to be coordinated, initially at least, through the state, in other words the idea was to replace one totality with another. I think what is happening now is that we are saying no, that is not the issue, the issue is how we detotalize, how we break that totality. Not in order to create another totality, but to create—perhaps, who knows how it's going to work out—at least for the moment, a multiplicity of social patterns or social cohesions. In other words, what we want is a world of many worlds. If you're into those debates, you can see it in terms of Adorno's critique of Lukács. Lukács was wonderful but he was into the Leninist party and saw things very much from the point of view of totality and that was the central category for him. Adorno's critique was No, absolutely not, that is really just to reproduce a repressive system. The issue now, I think, is not how do we replace one totality with another, but how do we detotalize, how do we actually think of a world that unleashes its energies or unleashes our creativity in different directions? How do we uncouple ourselves from the dynamic of death?

When we think of creating autonomies or autonomous spaces or cracks, what are the forces we come up against? The most obvious force is the violence of the state. I was being told a little while ago about the repression in Oakland or the repres-sion here, in San Francisco, the twelfth of October, was it? That is what the police are about: they are about trying to impose a social logic. That is what law and order means: it means, how do we make you fit into the system, how do we repress attempts to misfit collectively, how do we repress attempts to break the logic of the system?

But behind that, it seems to me, there is a greater force of social cohesion, which is the force of money or the force of value. Maintaining law and order is about how you maintain favorable conditions for investment in San Francisco. By keeping people quiet, by getting them off the streets, by not allowing San Francisco to acquire the image of a place of rebellion. But the real force behind the policing is the logic of money. How do we integrate San Francisco as favorably as possible into a world in which it is the logic of money that dominates, the logic of profit? Or, as Marx points out, if we want to understand this logic of money, we have to break the surface and see that this logic of money expresses the logic of value. And what value is about, what determines the magnitude of value, is the amount of socially necessary time of labor required to produce a commodity. Not just socially necessary labor time, but labor time of a particular type. Not just the amount of dancing or kissing or jumping up and down that is required to produce the commodity, but the amount of value-producing labor. In other words, the amount of abstract labor, the amount of alienated labor.

Behind the movement of money, behind the logic of money, is the logic of abstract labor. The logic that pushes our activity as humans into a certain form. It's important to come back to that, it's important to think—and that was the argument yesterday—our politics from ourselves, from our activity. One of the slogans over the last twenty, thirty years has been the idea of a politics of use value, to look at things in terms of their utility rather than in terms of their profitability. I think we have to go beyond that and say, "No, our strength isn't visible at the level of value; our strength is visible at the level of labor, at the level of the contradictory character of labor." At the level of not only our ability, but our daily practice of trying to break the logic of abstract labor all the time. Certainly, this logic poses all sorts of constraints and limits upon us, but we will not necessarily follow it, we will not necessarily make all our actions conform to that logic. Our real strength is in doing something else, in walking in the opposite direction. If we think not just of the problem of the police, behind that there is the more profound, more tightly integrated force which is the force of money, which is ultimately the force of abstract labor. If we ask how do we break that force, then we are beginning to get an answer by saying the way to break that cohesion is actually to do in a different way, to try and think from our own revolts against abstract labor. How can we break that logic?

Two points, just to finish—long points.

The first is that the social cohesion in which we live, this society, this tight weave within which we live, is obviously not total. At times we think it is, at times we think it's all domination, it's all money, that there's nothing that can be done. But the very fact that we perceive that domination, that we criticize it, means that that is not true. We can say, "Oh, we are special, we are the cleverest people in the world, that's why we can understand it." But if we don't want to say that, then we say, "Well no, the fact that we can see it actually indicates that that social cohesion is not as tight as it appears," that behind and beside that social cohesion is a constant movement against that cohesion. Behind money there is a constant movement against money; behind value there is a constant movement against value and for the creation of other values. If we think that, then we say, "We've been talking about that, the cracks. It's precisely what we've been saying, that the cohesion is not as tight as we thought." And then we think that the cohesion is not really a cohesion—it's not a noun, that's a false image—it's a verb, a cohering. It's a cohering, a kind of weaving together that is constantly going on, that is constantly tying us in. But We, at the same time, are constantly moving in the opposite direction. So then we begin to see that that means that money is a struggle. It's not a thing; it's a struggle to push us into certain forms of behavior. Value is not a thing; it's a struggle to push us into certain forms of behavior. Capital is not a thing; it pushes us into certain forms of action. And we begin to dissolve the world from being a world of nouns that weighs so heavily upon us and to think of the world as a world of verbs. And once we begin to think of the world as a world of verbs, we are beginning to open up spaces.

The other thing is that—and this is terrible but it is also a source of hope—if we think of this social cohesion or social cohering as being established through the form of money or through the form of value, then we can see that not only is it a constant struggle, but it is a constantly intensifying struggle. The significance of abstract labor or the significance of value production is not the same today as it was yesterday. That is fairly obvious if you think that if I were to make a car, for example, today in the same way as fifty years ago, would I be producing value? Of course not. It might be fun as a hobby, but you certainly wouldn't be producing something that would sell on the market, you wouldn't be producing value. To produce a car costs a lot less time today than it did fifty years ago. The meaning of abstract labor changes from day to day. The meaning of value production changes from day to day. The very fact that it is the socially necessary labor required to produce something that determines its value means that capital is a constant movement of faster, faster, faster and a constant extension of control over the whole of society, a constant tighter, tighter, tighter control.

On the one hand, that is awful because it means a constant process of dehumanizing, of humiliating, of pushing us down onto our knees, but it also means a constant process of rebellion. Not rebellion against something that is there; it's rebellion that grows out of resistance against an attack upon us. That is what is both horrifying about the situation, but it is also where hope lies, since capital won't let us sit still. Certainly, being a university professor today is nothing like it was when I first started teaching in the university. And that can be said, I think, of any job. The same for students. Writing a PhD today isn't at all the same as it was thirty years ago and that's because we suffer from this constant attack, this constant pressure. And that pushes us to rebel, that pushes us more and more to say "Ya Basta," to say more and more, "No, enough, this is insane. We have to do things in a different way, we have to walk in the opposite direction." It's this "faster, faster, faster," this "tighter, tighter, tighter control," this insatiable dynamic of capital that is in crisis today. The question then is, how do we understand that We are that crisis? And how do we think about the possibilities of revolutionary politics from that standpoint?

That's what I wanted to say today.

THREE

We Are the Crisis of Capital and Proud of It

In these three sessions we are trying to pose the question of how we can think about revolution after the failures of revolution in the twentieth century. It is not enough just to think of individual struggles. It is very important to focus on particular struggles, but we have to go further than that. We have to go further than that, because our problem is not just to win the occasional struggle and make things a little bit better here and there. Our problem is how we can break the dynamic of capitalism, the dynamic of money, the dynamic of profit, which is so obviously destroying the world and threatens to destroy humanity completely.

What I have suggested is that there is a shift taking place in the way that revolution is being posed. The dominant twentieth-century concept of revolution focused on the issue of conquering state power. The goal was to conquer state power and, from there, to bring about a major transformation in society. With the fall of the Soviet Union and the rise of China as a capitalist power, it has become very clear that that didn't work. So, if we want to go back to the question of revolution, we have to think of it in a different way.

The basic thing in the grammar or, perhaps better, anti-grammar, of revolution that is emerging is the idea that the central problem is not in the first place, or not only, exploitation, it is capital as a system of social cohesion. Capital as a system that increasingly draws all our activities into a certain logic—all our activities here, in the so-called more developed countries, but also all our activities throughout the world, into a certain logic, into the logic of profit. You can think of capitalism as a kind of spider's web that is gradually—or progressively, not gradually at all, actually very fast—strangling us all, pulling us into its logic, leaving no room for anything else, progressively destroying the world. The center of the web is, of course, the relation of exploitation, because the web wouldn't exist, this weaving of social relations through the dominance of money and commodity wouldn't exist if labor power itself weren't a commodity. It's not that we're throwing exploitation out the window, now we're going to talk about social cohesion, it's not that. Rather, there is a shift in the balance between these two central elements. What we are beginning to focus on is the notion of capital as a system of social cohesion. So then the question becomes not how we gain power in order to change everything but how we can break this system of social cohesion. That's the idea that has guided the way I have been thinking about these lectures. We started off on Tuesday with We, with the force of rupture, with the power that could potentially break the social cohesion, because the only way that we can break the spider's web is actually through the power of us flies, caught somewhere in the middle. In other words, we have to start with ourselves if we are going to think of a power of rupture. When we think of ourselves as the power, as the possible force of rupture, as the possible force that can push beyond capital, break this dynamic of death, then we are saying, in the first place, We are dignity. We will no longer accept this system based on humiliation, based on dehumanization, based on the negation of our own subjectivity, on the negation of our own dignity. We are dignity in revolt against the negation of our own dignity. We are dignified rage, *digna rabia*. We are not victims. If We start off thinking We are victims, then there is no way out, unless some kind of god or party comes along and saves us. And that's not going to happen.

When we start with the notion that We are dignity, We are not victims, We are not poor, We are rich in creative potential. We are rich because We are in fact the creators of the social world. We rise up not because We are poor but because We are rich. We are frustrated rich, because the richness of our creative potential is frustrated by the society We live in. Because our richness is forced into the commodity form, into the money form, into the prison of the commodity, of money. We are rich, We are the only creators, and therefore our lords and masters, the capitalists—capital, in other words—depend upon us. The lord always depends upon the servant and that is the source of hope.

We are in revolt because that is what dignity means, that is what humanity means, and there is absolutely nothing special about our revolt. We are in revolt because We are perfectly ordinary people. We are in revolt simply because to exist in a society based on domination means to struggle against that domination. And because We are in revolt and are ordinary and because We are dignity, We organize ourselves in ways that articulate our dignity, that articulate our rebellion, that articulate our struggle to take back the world. That means, I think, that we organize ourselves in assemblies, communes, councils, soviets, whatever you want to call them, and not in the form of the state, not in the form of state-centered organizations such as parties, because they are forms of organization designed to exclude us and which do effectively exclude us. We are dignity, We are richness, and We are also self-contradictory because We exist in, against, and beyond the existing society and that inevitably reproduces itself within us. So, We are self-contradictory and We are confused. We don't actually know all the right answers; We have questions. Asking, We Walk. We walk, We advance by asking, not by telling, not by laying down the correct answers, not by creating programs that everybody can follow.

And because We exist in and against and beyond the existing society, We are also anti-identitarian. The only way to actually conceive social change is by challenging our own identities, by moving beyond them, by negating them and going beyond. We are verbs, We are therefore anti-institutional. We overflow, We are verbs, not nouns and, crucially, We are doers, not laborers. We are, in fact, doers against labor. We are creators against the incarceration of our activity in the form of labor.

That's basically what I said the first day. For those of you who have been here the three days, that's the third time that you've heard it, but some things are worth repeating.

The second day I posed the question of revolution in terms of conflict between the forces of rupture, in other words ourselves on the one hand, and the forces of cohesion on the other hand. Then we focused on the following:

First of all, on the way in which our ruptures or pushes against and beyond are expressed and it seems to me that they are expressed volcanically, not smoothly, but in ruptures or eruptions all over the place. Spaces or moments or types of activity in which we say no, here we will not accept the logic of money, we will not accept the logic of profit, we will not accept the dynamic of death. Here, in this little space, in this little moment, in this particular activity—in relation to water, say, or education—we will not accept commodification. And these can be seen as cracks in the texture of domination, as autonomous spaces if you like, or they can be seen as dignities. Or they can be seen as communizings—spaces or moments in which we create the basis of what could possibly be another society.

Then we went on to talk about how these cracks confront an enormous force of social cohesion. This enormous force of social cohesion often makes its first appearance in the form of the police, who seek to enforce law and order. The law and order is, of course, the law and order of capital. Behind that first front of repression, there lies a deeper force of social cohesion, which is money. It is actually money that binds the world together, that binds our activities together. If we try to understand money, then we go to the concept of value, value as constituting the basis of money. Then we go a step further and see that what constitutes value is labor. What constitutes the magnitude of value of a commodity is the amount of labor time required to produce it. Once we get to labor, it's comforting. Well, it's not comforting at all; it's actually quite exciting, though, because then we are back home again. Once we say the basis of it all is labor, then we are on the home ground of our own activity. We are actually on the home ground of that which we control—or do not control, but could potentially control. Because when we talk about labor, the labor that creates value, the labor that therefore creates money and the social bond, we are talking about our own activity forced into a form that we do not control. In other words, we are talking about a tension that runs through our activity. Between the labor that we are forced to perform in order to click into this capitalist society, on the one hand, and that doing or creativity or longing against labor for a different sort of activity that runs deep inside all of us. Once we say this social cohesion is actually constituted by our own alienation, by our own alienation from ourselves, our own abstraction from ourselves, then we are immediately opening up another possibility and saying maybe we can actually give expression to the antagonism that is within our own activity, maybe there are ways in which we can say we will not labor. We will not subordinate our activity, at least not totally, to the dominion of capital.

If you think of those cracks I mentioned a moment ago, cracks like the Zapatista area in Chiapas, cracks like here, like CIIS, like this meeting, then this experience of going against labor, this experience of doing that which we consider desirable or necessary is actually a profound part of all our lives. If it's a profound part of all our lives, that means that anticapitalism is a profound part of all our lives, that there is nothing special about being anticapitalist. It's the most ordinary thing in the world, thank goodness.

The first day we talked about We and the second day we talked about capital as a system of social cohesion, and what I want to talk about today is We as the crisis of capital. As the crisis of this system of social cohesion. In other words, hence the title We Are the Crisis of Capital and Proud of It.

It's more common to understand crisis in the opposite way. It's more common to say the crisis is the fault of the banks or crisis is the fault of finance capital, or the fault of the government, they are the ones to blame: we're not to blame, they are in fact making us suffer for the consequences of their own irresponsibilities. That's a common theme in Left discourse here and throughout the world. That seems to me disastrous. Awful. First, because if we say they are the ones who are responsible for the crisis, we are being made to suffer the consequences, then we immediately put ourselves in the position of victims. And if we are victims, then what can we do except beg for a solution? We put ourselves in the position of supplicants. We say oh please, please, Mr. President, change the policies, create jobs for us, here we are waiting for your good will. That, for a start, seems to me to be wrong. But it's much worse than that in fact. Because if you say that the banks or the capitalists are to blame for the crisis, then there's something wrong. Because if capital is a form of domination, if capital is a relation of domination, then we are in effect saying that it's the dominators who are in the wrong: they are responsible for the crisis of domination. Please, let's get rid of them, let's put other bankers, other capitalists there, ones who are more competent, who can really dominate us effectively. I don't think that's what we want.

If we say capital is a relation of domination, then the obvious thing to say is if the relation of domination is not working properly, then that must be due to the dominated. It must be because the dominated—us, in other words—are not sufficiently submissive. That's why there is a crisis in the relation of domination. Once we think of that, then the whole question of politics, of how we think about the crisis, changes. But the question is, how can we think about that?

This idea was proposed by the autonomists or the *operaista* current in Italy in the 1960s and early to mid-1970s, and gradually spread. The argument was that we start the struggle of the working class. We understand that capital is the constant movement of trying to dominate the working class. We look at the crisis of the mid-1970s, the crisis of Fordism, and it is clear that that crisis is the result of the huge rise in struggles throughout the world from 1968 onwards. Not only student struggles, struggles of all sorts: struggles in the factories, struggles around the factories. And we conclude that the crisis of capital is due to the strength of working-class struggle. The problem now is that even if we still have the same analysis it is, at first sight, more difficult to maintain it in the present situation, just because we haven't had that sort of wave of obvious working-class struggle in the early years of this century. Certainly, there have been important struggles, but there hasn't been the same combination of social and factory-based struggles as there was in the late 1960s and early '70s. How do we maintain today that idea that the crisis of capital is due to us?

Yesterday we talked about capital as a system of social cohesion, but one crucial feature of capital that distinguishes it from all previous forms of domination is that it cannot stand still. It cannot be happy with dominating people the same way now as it dominated them ten years ago. There is a dynamic built into capitalist domination, which can be understood in terms of what constitutes value. Value is constituted by the socially necessary labor time required to produce a commodity and this socially necessary labor time is constantly falling, partly as human ingenuity expands. We find quicker ways of producing things. And that means that capital, capitalist domination, is based upon a constant movement of faster, faster, faster. If you produce something today, a car or a bicycle or a

PhD thesis, at the same pace as you produced it ten or twenty years ago, it will be no good, it won't sell, it won't have value. So there is this constant drive to produce things more quickly. The problem with that is that, if capital is all the time saying to us faster, faster, faster, then it inevitably comes up against our insubordination, our nonsubordination, our incapacity to subordinate ourselves sufficiently for the requisites of capital. Because, even if I'm a worker who really loves his boss, loves the company, says yes, I'm a faithful servant of my company, I will still always tend to assume that doing my job today in the same way as I did it yesterday will be all right. And of course it isn't and capital tells us, often in very violent ways, that it isn't. Inevitably, I think inevitably, we say, "No, that's not the way I did it yesterday. I have certain standards, certain ways of doing things, certain rhythms. I'm too old to learn new techniques." So, inevitably, capital and the constant acceleration that the existence of capital implies comes up against this force of nonsubordination or insubordination. I suppose that what I'm trying to suggest is that if you look at the present crisis, we can say that this crisis is to be understood not necessarily, or not only, in terms of open insubordination but in terms of the force of our incapacity or our refusal to subordinate ourselves sufficiently to the dynamic of capital.

I want to put in a footnote there, a footnote on autonomism or on autonomist theory, on the theory that was associated, in the first place, with the *operaista* movement in Italy but has spread throughout the world since then. I think what distinguishes my argument from what may now be called orthodox autonomist argument is that I think that autonomism traditionally emphasizes overt insubordination, overt struggle. It understands itself as a theorization of the world from the viewpoint of open struggle, from the viewpoint of open activism or open militancy. What I'm trying to say is that that is fine, but that we actually have to go beyond that and understand the world and the tendency to crisis not just on the basis of open insubordination, but on the basis of nonsubordination, on the basis of the nonsubordination that is an inherent part of everyday life. In other words, it's not that people necessarily proclaim themselves as activists, or become militants, or lead a strike, or lead a protest, or organize a march. It's very often that they just say, "Well, my back is hurting me today," or "I know I ought to go to work, but I'm going to stay at home and play with my children or look after my daughter who's ill." Or it could be just that "I love my boss, but I'm really not capable of or willing to put in the extra effort that would make my boss even more profitable than he is now." So, built into everyday experience there is this kind of reluctance, a dragging of feet, a refusal—this is perhaps the important thing—there is a refusal to accept that we are robots. There is a refusal to become robots, rather. There is a refusal to subordinate ourselves totally. Part of the argument—I only thought of it this afternoon, but I think it runs through the three talks—is that we have to think on the basis not only of insubordination, but from the basis of nonsubordination. And yet, if we think of us, if we think of us here in the room this evening, probably we are all in some way consciously insubordinate. It's not just that we are nonsubordinate, we are in some way consciously anticapitalist. Probably a lot of us think of ourselves as activists. I suppose what I'm saying is that we have to be careful—this is my criticism of mainstream autonomist theory—we have to be very careful to make sure that we don't understand our activism in terms of a contrast with the nonactivism of the people who are not here tonight. In other words, we have to try and think of our own activism or our own political engagement, let's call it, or our own engagement with the idea of changing society radically, in its continuity with the nonsubordination that characterizes the everyday life of everybody. Unless we think of ourselves in that way, unless we think of it in terms of that sort of continuity—that we are activists but our activism is simply the tip of an iceberg, or our activism is part of a subterranean stream of nonsubordination that runs through the whole of society—unless we think of it that way, then there is a great danger that we reproduce the vanguardism that we had probably started off by criticizing. We reproduce our own image of ourselves as somebody special, and obviously that would probably feed into the way that we relate to other people. That's why, for me, this question of thinking not just in terms of insubordination but in terms of nonsubordination and thinking in terms of the line of continuity between insubordination and nonsubordination seems very important. That was the footnote.

So, what I was arguing is that We, We in the broadest sense, constitute the crisis of capital simply because capital is not still. Capital is a constant aggression. Class struggle, if you like (or even if you don't like, and of course we don't like), class struggle comes from above. That seems to me fundamental as well, it seems to me completely wrong to think that we are the initiators of class struggle. No, class struggle comes from above; capital is a constant aggression. We respond and we overflow in our response. Capital is a constant aggression, we are constantly attacked, so the class struggle is not something we choose. It isn't We the militants are going out to fight the class struggle. No. We are actually all born into a world of class struggle because we are all constantly attacked by capital. And this is a constantly intensifying struggle on behalf of capital; it constantly demands more. When we say no—either we say no or we don't say no but we drag our feet—as a result the rate of profit falls. Then I think capital responds in two ways. Capital responds partly by confronting, by bringing in new managerial methods, by introducing new regulations in the universities and in the factories, the other factories, and partly, and perhaps overwhelmingly, what capital does is it flees. Capital flees constantly from its dependence upon labor, it flees constantly from its own incapacity to subordinate our activity sufficiently to the demands of abstract labor. And it flees, first of all, by flying into machinery. It says, "We'll solve the problem:

get rid of those nasty workers, we'll bring in machines to take their place and the machines will do exactly what we want. The machines won't go on strike, they won't stay at home just because their daughter is ill or whatever, the machines will obey us." So the first flight is into machinery, I suppose this is what is analyzed by Marx in *Capital*. He very explicitly says that machinery is introduced in order to impose order, in order to overcome the rebel hand of labor. But that doesn't really solve the problem, because you still have to use the workers to operate the machines. You don't have as many workers as before, but the workers have to produce enough value and enough surplus value not only to cover their own wages, but also to pay for the operation of the machinery and the cost of the machinery, and profit. And, unless you can greatly intensify the exploitation of the workers, then that doesn't happen. At least that is Marx's argument in his analysis of the tendency for the rate of profit to fall. Bringing in machinery doesn't solve the problem, it actually reproduces the tendency to crisis.

What happens then is, from the middle of the twentieth century, capital has a great idea. It finds a new way of fleeing. In effect, it says to itself, "Well, if we're not able to impose sufficient domination, sufficient submission in the production process, then we're going to pretend that we have done it. We'll just escape into a world of make-believe. We'll escape into a world of fiction. We'll escape into a world where we create more and more money, and the money doesn't have to correspond to real profit. That's OK, we'll escape into a world of credit." That's what happened. Keynes justifies it and when Keynes falls and the monetarists come in, then they don't justify it but they keep on doing it. And so there's an expansion of fictitious capital. There's this huge expansion which allows the system to carry on, allows capitals to function, allows as well a certain space for negotiation with the workers, saying, "If you really work hard then we'll give you better social benefits." It allows a space for negotiating with trade unions. Therefore, it also opens up a greater space for state-centered politics, for state-centered politics from the Left, because it opens up a space in which we can fight for minor changes and, perhaps, get them through the structures within the state system, through making demands of the state.

The problem with it is, of course, that it can't go on forever. It introduces the whole disconnection of money accumulation from the actual process of production, it opens up an enormous area of instability, and it becomes more and more difficult to maintain, until it expresses itself in financial crisis. And that is really what we have been living in throughout the world very openly, very explicitly, for the last four or five years. In this situation, the options for capital are limited. It still goes on fleeing, and it still goes on with a combination of confronting and fleeing, but more and more the fleeing becomes difficult, more and more the emphasis is on confrontation. "We won't negotiate. If you want to go on being unemployed, tough! If you're going to die of hunger, tough! If you can't get free medical benefits, tough!" And of course negotiation still goes on a bit, but the space for negotiation becomes more and more limited. I think what we're seeing at the moment, in Greece and Spain and Italy and in southern Europe in general, is the way in which this space for negotiation has been closed down. You get huge, huge demonstrations, which traditionally have been the basis for negotiations, and the demonstrations are just ignored completely. You get riots and you get the city center burnt down. In Athens in July 2011, they burnt down something like fifty-seven buildings in the city center. And the government says, "Well, we're not worried, we're OK. Let them riot, let them burn the city center down. We'll send out the police, bang them on their heads, let them live in misery." Or, what's her name, of the IMF, Christine Lagarde, she said, why should we worry about what's happening in Greece? Why should we worry about the disastrous fall in living conditions? Starving children in Africa are worse off than they are, so what's the problem?

In other words, it's complete closure. That's why there is an argument that we have entered an era of riots. Negotiation has closed down. It has been closing down progressively, I suppose, ever since the first years of neoliberalism, but what we're seeing at the moment and the last few years is a much tighter closing down of negotiation with the dominated. So there's a closure, an acceptance of riots. It is now assumed that of course parliaments or governments won't respond to the riots. What was so amazing, so completely outrageous last week in Cyprus was that the parliament actually listened to what the protesters were saying in the streets and said, at least at first, "No we won't, we won't accept the austerity package," which went completely against what parliaments have been doing in Europe over the last five years.

In that situation we have two options. If we say this is the core of the crisis, our refusal to subordinate ourselves sufficiently, to subordinate every aspect of our lives to capital, we are the core of the crisis. If we say that, then really there are only two possibilities, and I think these are the two possibilities that are present as a tension in all the anticapitalist movements at the moment, certainly in Spain, Greece, and Italy, and clearly in the Occupy movement here. There are two possibilities: one possibility is to say, "No, capital is to blame. We are totally willing to cooperate, we will subordinate ourselves. We know that if capital is to recover from its crisis then that is going to mean intensification of our subordination to capital. There is no other way in which capital can possibly recover, and that is what we want. Please, capital, please come back, please exploit us more effectively, please, above all, give us jobs." That, of course, is part of the movement. We want employment, we want to be employed, we want to be exploited. We know what exploitation means, we know that any postcrisis capitalism will be based on an intensification of that exploitation, but we have to live, we want jobs! Please, come back, capital. Please let us return to normal domination.

And the other possible response is to say, "No, that's not what we want. We are the crisis of capital and proud of it. We are the crisis of this relation of domination. We are the possibility of another way of living, of another form of social organization. Therefore we do not want domination to overcome its crisis; we do not want capital to overcome its crisis. We want this to be the last crisis of capital. We want to create a world that is no longer dominated by capital, that is no longer subject to the logic of money, to the logic of profit, to the dynamic of death." And we point politely to the garbage can over there in the corner and we say, "Please, capital, go and deposit yourself in your proper place." We see that capitalism has failed. I think this is what is clear in the present crisis, what is being said more and more, especially in those countries that are in the paroxysm of the crisis. They are saying that capital has failed. Move over, capitalism, let's create something else. And that's the other side of the whole movement of the last few years, Occupy, indignados, etc.: to say no, we don't want to go back to exploitation.

My favorite example is the example of the Unemployed Workers' Association in Solano, on the outskirts of Buenos Aires. In Argentina there was a huge unemployed workers' movement from about 1995 onwards, where they blocked the roads all over the country and called for the government to introduce subsidies for the unemployed, which hadn't existed, and also to create jobs. And they were extremely effective. And then some of the most radical groups began to say, "Well, maybe that's not really what we want. We've had jobs in the past, we're not really too enthusiastic about going back to work in McDonalds or going back to work in the factory. That's not actually what we want to do with our lives. What we want to do is to do what has meaning for us. We want to do that which makes sense for us. We want to improve our communities, to help each other, we want to create community kitchens, to create community workshops, to create community schools."

And they said, "No, we don't want to go back to work." They were one of the most articulate groups, the group of Solano. And that's what they did. They said, "Fine, yes, we do want subsidies, but we want these subsidies as a collective, and we will decide what to do with the subsidies. Of course part goes to the people in need but also we will use part of it collectively on the projects that we want."

I think that is the dilemma that has been facing the movement over the last few years. Do we say, "Please, please, please, we want jobs," or do we say, "No, we actually want to create something different"? And I think that, certainly in Greece and in Spain, the movement to say, "No, this is not a movement about more employment; this is a movement against capitalism, a movement to create alternatives," has been extremely strong. And they have been doing all sorts of things, but my favorite example, my favorite crack of all is Navarino Park, which is in the center of Athens. In the riots that followed the police killing of a fifteen-year-old in December 2008, riots for days all over Greece, and in Athens they went into a car park and they tore down the walls and created a garden, there, in the center of Athens. It is a community garden and they have swings and things for children to go and play, and people go and talk and sit there, and they grow vegetables, and they organize concerts and talks, and they discuss how to struggle against capitalism, how to create the basis for a different society, which is just beautiful.

And this sort of thing has been happening, I think, all over Greece and all over Spain; people are being forced to create alternatives. It is to some degree by choice, but people are being forced to develop other ways of living, other forms of social relations simply in order to survive. That is the dilemma that confronts us. Which way do we go? If we want to talk about revolution, then there is no question. Revolution means not asking for capital to come back. Revolution means breaking the system, means developing alternative forms of living. It means communizing and developing all sorts of communizings. The only question is, can we do it?

My own feeling is that if we look at what is happening in Greece and Spain, then probably for the moment no, we can't do it. Perhaps for the moment we cannot say, "Just go to hell, capital." It's very difficult. For the moment we probably don't have the capacity to survive completely without capitalist things. We are caught in a contradictory situation, and I think that is the experience for all those who are involved in autonomist groups. People have to find some way of surviving. They can say what we really put our energy into is creating alternative radio stations, skill exchanges, or gardens. We really put our energy into developing forms of security that come from ourselves and don't depend on the police—security against the police, safety against the police.

But, at the same time, we are often caught in the contradictory situation that we have to earn a wage or a salary, if we're able to do it, or find some form of funding, some form of financial sustenance. It's probably best to recognize that we are actually caught in this contradictory situation.

How, from here, do we go forward? Partly by asking, by discussing, by trying to think together, by meeting, by having assemblies or whatever. But I think as well we go forward by hoisting a flag. We say, "Well, we can't do at the moment exactly what we want, we can't get rid of capital completely. It will take us a little while, but we can hoist flags all over the place; we can hoist the flag of communizing, of creating the basis for a society with a completely different form of organization." I suppose this is what we are doing here. Today I was in a meeting with the people from Unitierra, of California. That's the idea. Here, in this space, we are hoisting the flag of doing something else, of walking in the opposite direction. We can create gardens, we can campaign to stop foreclosures and to stop the enforcement of debt, we can organize collectively against the enforcement of debt, we can create alternative radios, pirate radios, we can share software, share music, we can occupy factories—we can do all that, and we are doing all that. That's what's so exciting.

One of my favorite slogans from the Occupy movement was something I saw in a photo of the general strike in Oakland, a placard saying, "The Beginning Is Near." But that's not quite right. It's not that the beginning is near, it's rather that we have already begun. And that's why we're here and thank you very much.

Andrej: OK, so let's take three questions.

Q: *My question is about that being caught in a contradictory situation. I'm wondering if different communities, as they face this contradictory situation, have different cultural and political resources. We've been talking about the Zapatistas for the last three days and thinking about the Caracol and the Junta, but at the same time we're also talking about a* sistema de cargo, *a* sistema de tequio *as various kinds of technologies that come from five hundred years of struggle, as a cultural and political resource.*

Q: *It seems to me you've done the big bang not enough service. And I'm alluding to Chapter 17 in* Crack Capitalism, *where you acknowledge that there's the material universe, as distinct from stuff made by human beings. Plants, nature . . . And I'd like you to speak to that. And what I mean by that, to be a little clearer with the audience here, is the . . .*

J: You mean that you think there are some people who haven't yet arrived to Chapter 17?

Q: *Yes! I mean that most of us live in a binary way of thinking: that there's capital and labor. And there is a trinitarian way of looking at the world, and that's that there is nature, and there is capital, and there is labor. And I'd like you to address that third* *element as a distinct aspect of the debt crisis we're in. It's about locational value, debt. I paid $500,000, for instance, to buy my piece of San Francisco, and most of that $500,000 in debt is for the location, it's not for the building. Right?*

Q: *I think about how we created capitalism in the first place, so that's another part of it, but I'm sure that many of us, including myself, have been involved in trying to make cracks and community projects and collective projects, and a lot of these projects have succeeded to some extent, but what happens over and over again is individual human beings have conflict with each other, and a lot of times that conflict breaks apart whatever the project is, and it happens over and over and over again, so human beings have in us flaws that . . . How do we deal with that? It comes up so much.*

J: I'd like to start with the last question. First, your point about how we created capitalism in the first place. I think it's not just a question of how we created capitalism in the first place, but how we create capitalism in the second place, in the third place, in the fourth place, how we create capitalism today, and how, possibly, we will create capitalism tomorrow. In other words, if capitalism exists, it's not because it was created a couple of centuries ago. If capitalism exists it is because we create it and recreate it. If it exists today, it's because we created it today, and if we don't create it tomorrow then it won't exist tomorrow. In other words, the problem of revolution . . . I mentioned yesterday, but very briefly, the question of time and how thinking of cracks or the change in the grammar of revolution that's taking place, crucially involves a change in the concept of time. Part of that is the realization that we do or do not create capitalism each day. The problem of revolution is not how we abolish this great monster that confronts us, which is capitalism. The problem of revolution is how we stop making capitalism tomorrow, or today in fact.

I know that wasn't exactly your question, but . . . The question . . . Yes, that has been my experience as well. That these attempts to create other things often, not always, but do frequently end up in the most awful conflicts. I certainly wouldn't say that, therefore, this is an aspect of human nature. I think that these things tend to happen in moments of stagnation. As long as the movements are moving—movements that don't move aren't really movements—as long as there is a development, as long as there is a connecting up with other movings, then on the whole the situation will be much more productive.

One of the things I emphasized yesterday was the notion of a crack. The reason why I use the metaphor crack is to think in terms of something that is constantly on the move. Once a crack stops moving and becomes a closed autonomous space, then I think it loses its dynamic, I think it loses its significance as a crack, and I think that is when conflicts start to arise and intensify.

The first point about the Zapatistas and the different resources, yes, I think that's important. If we think of the Zapatistas and their amazing ability to rise up, to involve a huge number of people in a constant process over a very long time, almost twenty years publicly, almost thirty years since they started, it is extraordinary. The ability to do that, I think, has a lot to do with the traditions that existed in those communities before the Zapatistas came into being. It has a lot to do with traditions, it has a lot to do with community solidarity, it has a lot to do with habits of working together, at least in certain situations. Obviously, we cannot simply decree the same traditions into existence, let's say in the context of the city. But everywhere there are certain traditions and certain patterns of working together, certain patterns of solidarity, certain patterns of mutual support, even in the most apparently individualized society. It's no good wishing that we too were an indigenous community in Chiapas; we have to start from where we are. We are where we are and we have to move on from there.

The other question about nature. I spoke briefly about the duality of and the antagonism between doing and abstract labor, or between what Marx calls concrete labor and abstract labor. In the book I suggest that the abstraction of doing, the abstraction of our activity into abstract labor or the conformation of our activity as alienated labor is not just the basis of a certain way of acting; it also affects fundamentally the way in which we relate to one another and the way in which we think, and it affects, crucially, our relation with nature. It gives rise to an objectification of nature, to a treatment of nature as a thing, and the treatment of other forms of life as a thing. Part of the great movement at the moment, the great diversity of movements, of rebellions against the current dynamic is the questioning of that separation, the questioning of the treatment of nature as an object, the attempt or multiple attempts to recover our relation to nature and to recover and recompose our relation to other forms of life: to rethink the whole question, not just in terms of society but in terms of understanding our human nature as part of natural relations as a whole. You can see that, for example, in the importance of all sorts of ecological movements, of gardening movements, the creation of community gardens, the creation of other gardens that try to recapture or re-form, rather, the relation with nature. That doesn't give an exact answer to the cost of the location of your house in San Francisco, but I do think that the rethinking of our relation with nature and our relation with other forms of life is absolutely crucial for the process of communizing or communizings.

Q: *You were talking earlier about the space in negotiation increasingly decreasing, and you named Cyprus last week as a specific example of that, that what was amazing about it being that the government listened and responded, so I'm curious if you've* noticed certain things in place in that context that allowed that to occur. Do you see an exception or are there certain components in place that allow for that listening to happen?

Q: Hi, John, nice to see you. This is Chris Carlsson.

J: Oh, hi, Chris!

Q: *Thanks for referencing* Nowtopia *in your book, I was very honored by that. I really love that you're carrying on the conversation around nonsubordination and the notion of overflowing, and that space being what causes the crisis of capital, because I really agree with that and I kind of sheepishly have to think, "Oh, does that mean that here in San Francisco, where there seems to be some kind of weird economic boom going on, we're all very good and subordinate?" Because here it seems to be functioning quite well, even though plenty of people here are miserable as well.*

But the question I wanted to get to is more—you did reference that in your book—about science and technology being one of these areas that can be a potential crack of a conflict, and that's something I've been fascinated by and interested in, that there is an epistemological shift that's going on amongst a lot of people. In a broad way, society knows much more today than we have ever known before about biology, ecology, the reproduction of life, and to put it simply, what you are arguing for is that we can get up tomorrow and make the world very differently than what we do today. But one key element of that is convincing ourselves that we can reproduce a complex society. And you use a lot the language of rupture and breaking and anti-institutionalization, and I'm both enthused about that and then I think, well, but so many people, that scares the hell out of them. Because they feel, well, if we're going to break everything, how is the water going to get here and how is electricity going to keep running? I realize this is kind of flying in several directions at the same time. I'm a little bit confused, but this notion of the general intellect, which I don't think you mentioned tonight but I believe you bring it up at least briefly in your book, and of course it is part of the whole autonomy thread, and this is kind of what I tend to think as one of the key elements of what we're up to right now, is the appropriation of technological and scientific knowledge at the base of society, and its reconceptualization on a new basis as a way of reproducing life every day. So I thought I'd throw all that at you and see what you have to say about it.

Q: *One of the reasons why I am confused by your argumentation is who is considered within the We? Who is the we that is complicit in the creation of capital, because as a white person with the privilege of living in a big area, I understand how I may be complicit, but I'm not quite understanding those that have been born under the domination and colonization, and communities of color, specifically, like in the USA and so on. And then, with that question in mind, seeing how at the end of your entry you say it's not that moment now, so what we can do now is to raise flags of different sort of projects—community building, whatever that may look like—but I'm afraid of what that means for white liberals and how that actually doesn't make sense in solidarity with deconstructing capitalism and challenging capitalism in meaningful ways that actually change the lives of those that are enslaved under it, that are enslaved to my complicity with it.*

J: The first question, Sarah's question about Cyprus. I don't really know. I don't know enough about Cyprus. Certainly when the Cypriot parliament first threw out the measures proposed by the president, I think my reaction was, What is wrong? How can we suddenly find a parliament that seems to be responding to the demonstrations in the streets? When, if you think of Greece, you have massive demonstrations right outside the parliament and the parliament just didn't listen at all. I don't know. Maybe because it's a small place, maybe because they were caught by surprise and hadn't yet thought out what it really means to be a parliamentarian. I don't know.

Chris's point about science and technology. Yes, I think I agree. Well, it was a question, I don't know how I can agree to a question! It's a bit too easy, isn't it? I think two things. I think I'm more and more convinced, and this is something I want to think out, it kind of comes up in *Crack Capitalism*, but I really feel more and more the need to think out the question of productive forces and how we rethink the whole concept of productive forces, and how we go back to the old concept that was so central to the Marxist tradition of the relation between productive forces and the relations of production. Understanding those productive forces not as technology, not as machinery, not as progress, but as our own creative capacity. And yes, that certainly means trying to understand the importance within that context of science and technology. And the importance within that context of the historical continuity of the We, how We are interrelating, not only with the doings or activities of people who are alive but also with the activities and achievements of people who are dead. One thing that I discuss more in *Change the World* is the importance of the concept of thinking in terms of a social flow of doing or a flow of social doing. The way in which, once we begin to think of our own activities, we see that they are completely inseparable from the whole social flow of doing that constitutes human achievement, if that's the right word.

On the question of the institutions and the idea that to say we are anti-institutional is a bit frightening: my idea is that we probably, at the moment, do not have the capacity to live with the intensity of what a fully communist society would involve. This is something that Adorno says as well, to think of a society where we don't have institutions or identities to hold on to is a vertiginous thought. Maybe we're not ready yet, maybe in some way we do actually need institutions or some sort of patterns of practices in order to be able to cope with living. But, at the same time, I think that we can say that all these established practices and patterns and institutions are limits on freedom and therefore are limits on the development of our capacity to create. Therefore, at the same time as we may need some sort of institutional framework for our own poor sanity, we are actually committed to fighting against it.

And the third question about We and who are We and the difficulties of We. When I did the summary at the beginning today, I gave this list of We are, We are, We are. But I did start off on Tuesday by saying that, in the first place, We are a question. It's not that We are an identity, we don't know who We are. It seems to me important for two or three reasons.

First, because We is a concept which is being used more and more by anticapitalist movements. More and more they are saying We—without defining that We—they are not saying the working class is, or the downtrodden are. They are saying We are. And I think that opens the question.

Second, I think it's important to say We because we have to break the third person. The third person is the third person of domination, the third person is the grammar of domination. The third person involves the objectification of people, the definition of people as being other than ourselves.

And I think that We is also important because we have to start with our own problems. Wherever we are in this society or wherever we are in terms of thinking of social change, we have to start from We. It seems to me dishonest not to start with We. In other words, if we start off a book or a sentence saying, "the working class is" or "those people are" or "the capitalists are," we are hiding ourselves from view. We are not actually posing ourselves up-front as the problem that we know we are. My We is very much a question. And it's a question with lots of problems, because of course then you can say, "Well yes, but this We is actually hiding all this fragmentation that is enormously important." I would agree with that up to a point, except my We also is based on the idea that there is something we share in one way or another, which is our negated dignity. Certainly, the negation of our dignity takes place in many different ways. For many people, it means virtual slavery; for other people it involves working in the factory; for other people it means being tied to the home; for other people it means being processed through universities. There are lots of forms that this negation of dignity takes. But, for me, the We is the recuperation of dignity fighting against its own negation. With lots of problems.

Q: *I always appreciate good political analysis, but an instance I experienced today made me think that perhaps we also need good psychological analysis, if not good psychotherapy. I don't know if you saw the first movie of* The Matrix, *but I thought it was wonderfully metaphorical and it was actually good psychological analysis about a political phenomenon, and I will say whatever the screenwriters of* The Matrix *actually intended, I reinterpreted it to be that the majority of Americans is psychologically dependent upon this Republicrat system that we have. And for people who call themselves liberals or progressives or leftists psychologically depended on the Democrat party or the Democrat fraction of the Republicrats. I mean, we have what some African American friends of mine call Seeking the Biracial Savior, in Obama, which I've always regarded as the ultimate facelift on American imperialism and international neoliberalism. So, what it seems to be here, it seems to me, a psychological dependence on the establishment by people both ordinary and famous, at least amongst progressives, people like Michael Eric Dyson, Cornel West, other people of that stature who are actually longtime casual friends of mine, this desire, basing one's self-esteem on a desire to belong to at least the so-called liberal—what I recall—faction of the Republicrats, or as Dyson said in a debate with Glen Gore, you're either in the tent or you're not in the tent. I mean about the Democrat party tent. And if you're not in the tent, you can't participate. Now, why my friends Michael Eric*

Dyson or Cornel West, or to a certain extent even someone like Noam Chomsky would even want to be in that tent and base their personal self-esteem on participating in the liberal faction of the establishment. We can rationalize. I can say I do or don't understand, but I'm wondering what your response—if you have one based on the premise of my—to where so many Americans place their self-esteem. Those who are liberal place their self-esteem on wanting to participate in that sort of establishment as opposed to saying, No, that's not the tent we want to be in and we don't need to base our self-esteem on it.

Q: Hi there. One of the things you spoke about earlier and I think maybe even from yesterday was likening our ruptures to volcanic eruptions. And, given that, I think I would just like to hear a little bit more about the nature of struggles that we're seeing that are erupting in different times and different places with different intensities and which we may not have a very close connection to. I don't feel like I'm very connected to what's happening in Cyprus, other than the larger liberal project that is being responded to. And the fact that the eruption and the anticipation happen in different time frames makes it also hard to keep the continuity. I'm not really wanting to ask you how do we do it, but I do want to have a little bit more insight from you around keeping the momentum going. That momentum is kind of what drives us and what enables that kind of push-against to erupt in a sense. How can we, those of us who do very localized and site-specific and situation-specific—you know, my own situation and then working to rebel against how that fits into a capitalist notion—how do we connect them globally? Because we have these global systems. It's a little bit about local-global and also continuing momentum.

J: On the first question, one of the things—I mentioned it just briefly but I emphasized it more the first day—is that I think we have to start off from the realization that we are inherently schizophrenic. Schizophrenic, at least, in the popular sense of being self-antagonistic. That we have contradictory ideas, that our ideas move from one moment to another, that our ideas and our actions are in conflict. The Left tradition tends to think of an "us" who are revolutionary and a "them" who are integrated into the system. I don't think it's like that at all. I think that if we think in those terms, there's not much way in which we can move forward, because in the best of cases that means that we must convince *them*, we must tell *them*, how things really are. We've done that, we've tried that, and it didn't work. We have to think, rather, in terms of these contradictions being within all of us, so that your friends who are happy to be in the Democratic tent, as you put it, on some level they must also be unhappy with that. At some level, we are trying to address the contradictions within people. The other day, earlier on, when I was talking about the nonsubordinate, rather than the insubordinate, that is of huge relevance for the way we think about politics and the way we think about the possibility of revolution, because it means then that we recognize in the nonsubordinate a hidden insubordination of which they may or may not be conscious. When we talk about rebelliousness or revolution, we are trying to touch that insubordination within them, we are trying to bring it to the light, we are trying to make that which is invisible visible to us and visible to them. We're trying to make it visible, we're trying to articulate it or encourage its articulation. It really has to do with two other things that I was going to mention and I didn't.

One is the idea that came up in the discussion last night of things being on the tip of people's tongue. It came up in the discussion of hope and whether to talk of hope is not a privilege of this society, whether to talk of revolution or indeed of critique is not a privilege. I was saying that I think that no, in fact, it's ridiculous; it doesn't make sense to think that we can bring hope to people, or that we can bring critique to people, or that we can bring consciousness to people. Rather, what we try to do in the best of cases is to draw or help people to articulate the rebelliousness that is already within them, the hope that is already within them. And that means that what we are trying to do, we the people who sit here on the table, or we as theorists or intellectuals or whatever we are, I'm not sure what we are, but what we're trying to do is to formulate what is on the tips of people's tongues, that which they do not quite express, which they do not quite give articulation to.

It also has to do with something else that is one of my favorites, the initial reaction to the Zapatista uprising. In the first book of communiqués by the Zapatistas, there is an intro-duction by the historian Antonio García de León, in which he says, "As we heard or read these communiqués coming in one day after another, we gradually came to realize that in fact this rebellion was something that was rising up from inside us," coming up from our guts. That's the point, isn't it? That's the argument against the third person as well: it's not that it's a rebellion of them; it's actually our rebellion. It's something that is there, inside us. That's why we're here tonight. That's why people live, that's what makes people human.

The question of volcanoes. I'm very keen on volcanoes, partly because I live just beside a volcano, Popocatépetl, near Puebla, which is live and constantly smoking. Volcanoes seem to me important; it's this idea of something that we contain, a rebellion within us. We contain a revolt within us that then does come out—it explodes. It explodes individually and it explodes socially in different times and different places. You can think of a social flow of rebellion running through the world and that actually explodes, let's say in 1994 in Chiapas and in 2001 in Argentina and 2006 in Oaxaca and 2008 in Athens and 2011 in Spain and Greece, etc. In other words, there is flow of rebel-lion, constantly on the move. There's a unity, connections, and people are often conscious of the connections, but the explo-sions themselves are difficult to predict. It is a kind of bursting out from inside us collectively. And they are probably always responses to the aggressions of capital.

How do you keep the momentum going? I suppose part of that idea is that you don't. Or that you may do, but that perhaps we shouldn't put too much emphasis on continuity, that we shouldn't put too much emphasis on keeping the momentum going. If you think these are explosions of anger, explosions of creation, it doesn't necessarily mean that they are going to last more than a week or more than a year or more than ten years or twenty years, and their success or importance doesn't necessarily depend on their continuity. They can be important as moments of creation, as great fireworks that light up the sky and change the way we think and change the way that we see the world and open up new ways and new perspectives.

Andrej: OK, we have time for one more question.

Q: *I'm wondering if you can say more about the relationship between the We and the overflow. So, for example, you said we overflow in our response to capitalism. And I'm wondering, do you see the We and the overflow as, for example, temporally related? Do they occur at the same time? Are they constitutive of each other; are they grammatically related as one is a verb, the other is a noun? If you can say more about that relation.*

J: For me, We are the overflow. We overflow. We misfit. We misfit because we have no choice. Because capitalism is a system into which we cannot fit. We cannot fit because we don't fit in, because we are not yet robots. Robots, I think, wouldn't have a problem of misfitting. Robots fit, they're fine. Robots are identitarian, they Are. And we have not yet, at least, become robots. So we still misfit, so we overflow whatever category. Robots are nouns. We are verbs. We are verbs because we move, because we overflow, because we are not yet. Because our not-yet-ness pushes us all the time beyond where we are. As I said a minute ago, We is a question. That's the difference, for me, between the first person and the third person.

The third person is contained. If you talk about the working class as a third person, you are already beginning to define them. You are beginning to say there they are, and they can only reach a certain degree of consciousness; as Lenin said, they could only reach trade union consciousness. The very third-personization of the working class already restricts it. If you say We, and if we say We are a question, We are a question because We are on the move, because We overflow, because We break bounds, and because if you think of our antagonism with capital as being our antagonism with the system of social cohesion, then you can say that what capital does is to force us into a certain form of cohesion, a certain identity, a certain synthesis if you like. But We are the movement that breaks the cohesion, that breaks the synthesis, that breaks identities. We overflow because we are human.

Bibliographical Note

Who is there, standing at my shoulder, prompting me, giving me ideas, at times disagreeing? Obviously nobody who speaks or writes is expressing ideas that she or he has created from nowhere. The justification for footnotes, however heavy or pedantic they may become, is that they are an open acknowledgement of these hidden friends. The text published here originated as three talks, so there were no footnotes. So who was there sitting beside me as I spoke? My friends and students, of course. Perhaps most of all the fortnightly seminar that I started with Sergio Tischler in Puebla more than fifteen years ago, where with friends, students, and passers-by we just go reading through and arguing about whatever books we want to read and argue about. Some authors are there all the time in our discussions: Bloch, Adorno, Marx—and of course the Zapatista experience is always there as background.

And so for my bibliographical essay: read the Zapatista communiqués, read Ernst Bloch's *The Principle of Hope*, read Adorno's *Negative Dialectics*, and most of all, read Marx's *Capital.* Read it as struggle. Read it from struggle. Read it from Ayotzinapa.

Read it from Ayotzinapa. At this moment, early 2015, all thought starts from Ayotzinapa. Ayotzinapa, where the police disappeared forty-three students four months ago and killed three more. Ayotzinapa, where the hunt for the students has so far led to the identification of the body of just one of them, and to the discovery of hundreds more bodies in clandestine mass graves. Ayotzinapa as concentrated horror. But Ayotzinapa too as a tremendous wave of ¡Ya Basta! Enough! Enough of this system of violence, inequality, exploitation! Enough of this system which people are treated as things.

Ayotzinapa is Guantánamo is Palestine is the war in Iraq is the growing disparities between rich and poor is, is, is, is ... what seems to be the whole history of humanity. And when will the criminals be punished, when will we see the incarceration of Peña Nieto, Bush, Cheney, Blair, Kissinger, Obama, Merkel, Putin, Slim, Gates, and so on and on and on?

How, then, do we dare to hope for a better world? How do we, the losers of always, dare to hope? That is the central question of *Capital*. How can we understand current society as struggle? How can understand current society as a struggle that we might win? How can we understand current society as a struggle from which we might be able to create a different world?

This is not an empty wishful thinking that comes out of the air. It is a desperately urgent question that comes from the fact that we are being attacked. It comes to us just as surely as a person surrounded by attackers on a dark night thinks, how can I get out of here? The attack comes in the very first line of *Capital*: "The wealth of those societies in which the capitalist mode of production prevails presents itself as 'an immense accumulation of commodities'" (1965, 35). That is the key to the aggression against us, Marx suggests. Our wealth, our richness, that which we create, "the absolute working-out of [humanity's] creative potentialities, with no presupposition other than the previous historic development, which makes this totality of development, i.e. the development of all human powers as such the end in itself, not as measured on a *prede-termined* yardstick? Where he does not produce himself in one specificity, but produces his totality? Strives not to remain something he has become, but is in the absolute movement of becoming?" as Marx puts it in the *Grundrisse* (1973, 488). This creativity which is the absolute movement of our becoming (how could he put it more beautifully than that?) is reduced to an immense collection of commodities, of things outside us, of things to be bought and sold. What could be more violent than that? The "complete working-out of the human content appears as a complete emptying-out" (ibid.).

We long for a different world, then, not just because of particular injustices or horrors like Ayotzinapa or Guantánamo, but because we realize that these horrors are part of an aggressive structuring of the world in which that which makes us human, the absolute movement of our becoming, is turned against us, a world in which our richness exists an immense collection of commodities.

But our question is not "why do we hope for a different world?" but a much more difficult one: what makes us think that we have a real chance of breaking capitalism and creating this different world? The answer is not obvious, as well we know. Marx shows in *Capital* that the commodity is the keystone of an immense structure or totality of oppressive social relations. The commodity comes to dominate society only when our very core, our creative power, becomes a commodity (being transformed in the process from creative power into labor power): in other words, when we are forced by circumstances (our separation from the means of creating richness) to sell our labor power to someone who controls those means (the capitalist) so that they can exploit it to increase their wealth. The violence of the commodity is anchored in the daily repeated process of exploitation, which makes the powerful more powerful, the rich richer, a process that has its own dynamic, beyond all human control: "Accumulate! Accumulate! That is Moses and the prophets!" This drive to accumulate assaults all that stands in its way: communities, relations between children and their parents, the ecological conditions necessary for human reproduction. The drive to accumulate is a constant attack against other ways of weaving social relations, against all that stands in the way of the rule of money, of profit.

Yet that is not the question. Our question is not "how do we understand the terribleness of capitalism?" Just the opposite. With our eyes open to that terrible dynamic and its coherent drive to destruction, how do we nevertheless dare to hope? How do we understand the weakness, the fragility of capitalism? In other words, the central issue is crisis. For me, Marxism is important because it is a theory of the crisis of capitalism. It is not that it *has* a theory of crisis; it *is* a theory of crisis. It sees capitalism from the perspective of its mortality, from the standpoint of the weakness at its core. That is announced in the first sentence of *Capital*, which we have already quoted: "The wealth of those societies in which the capitalist mode of production prevails appears as 'an immense collection of commodities.'" This not only tells us of the aggression of the commodity form (an aggression which quite literally kills thousands and thousands of people each day), it also tells us of a richness that does not fit, that is not entirely contained within the commodity form, for otherwise we would have no way of seeing it there. Richness stands as the beautiful worm in the poisonous apple of capital. And we are that richness.

For the struggle against capitalism, the importance of Marxism, and hence the importance of reading *Capital*, is that it is a theory of crisis and hence an answer to the question "how do we dare to hope?" No other form of radical theory is a theory of crisis. Anarchism, feminism, ecologism, and so on present important ways of understanding oppression and of struggling against it, but they do not understand that oppression from the perspective of its mortality, of its crisis.

Of course that is not the way that *Capital* has been traditionally understood. It is often understood as simply providing an analysis of how capitalism works and the theory of crisis is seen simply as one aspect of this working, or, in some versions, as being the basis of a theory of collapse, but a collapse understood as separate from the movement of struggle. In other words, the dominant interpretation of *Capital* has been a structuralist interpretation, which sees its contribution to struggle (if this is considered relevant at all) as being an analysis of the *framework* within which struggle takes place. In practice there is a growing distance between active anticapitalist struggle and the reading of *Capital*: hence my bibliographical plea to read it again, not as an analysis of the framework of struggle but as an analysis of struggle.

This means putting ourselves in the center of the reading, and it means understanding contradiction as antagonism. Read from Ayotzinapa. Read from our own anger, from our own dignity. When we read that richness exists in the form of the commodity, when it sinks in what that means and the death and the misery it involves, we scream with anger, with the rage of entrapped dignity. The dignity is there, our richness, entrapped but also not entrapped, not entirely contained, existing in but also against-and-beyond the commodity form, as struggle, as creative experiment. The relation between richness and the commodity is not just one of contradiction, it is an antagonism, a live struggle, involving police, teachers, parents, psychologists, perhaps all of us on the one side, and on the other side all of us too, the misfits, the rebels. An antagonism that cuts through all of us, an antagonism that confronts us every day as dilemma, as life-choice. Our rage burns within us as the rage of entrapped dignity: rage against the society that entraps us, rage against ourselves that construct the society that entraps us. And then, when a few pages later, we read that "the two-fold nature of the labour contained in commodities [as concrete and abstract labour] . . . is the pivot on which a clear comprehension of Political Economy turns" (1965, 41), then it begins to click for us, then we recognize that this rage that burns in-and-against-and-beyond us is the fury of the active principle of richness, what Marx calls (unfortunately) "concrete labour," our doing, our creativity, the absolute movement of our own becoming. Then too we recognize that it is the force of the absolute movement of becoming that constitutes the crisis of capitalism, that is the only possible answer to the question "How do we, the losers of always, dare to hope?"

But this is just a bibliographical note. I am not going to spoil the story by telling it all to you. Go and read *Capital*.

References

Adorno, Theodor W. *Negative Dialectics*. London: Routledge, 1990. Originally published 1966.

Bloch, Ernst. *The Principle of Hope*. 3 vols. Cambridge: MIT Press, 1986. Originally published 1954–1959.

Marx, Karl. *Grundrisse*. London: Penguin, 1973. Written 1857–1858, originally published 1939.

Marx, Karl. *Capital*, Vol. 1. Moscow: Progress Publishers, 1965. Originally published 1867.

ABOUT PM PRESS

PM Press was founded at the end of 2007 by a small collection of folks with decades of publishing, media, and organizing experience. PM Press co-conspirators have published and distributed hundreds of books, pamphlets, CDs, and DVDs. Members of PM have founded enduring book fairs, spearheaded victorious tenant organizing campaigns, and worked closely with bookstores, academic conferences, and even rock bands to deliver political and challenging ideas to all walks of life. We're old enough to know what we're doing and young enough to know what's at stake.

We seek to create radical and stimulating fiction and non-fiction books, pamphlets, T-shirts, visual and audio materials to entertain, educate, and inspire you. We aim to distribute these through every available channel with every available technology—whether that means you are seeing anarchist classics at our bookfair stalls, reading our latest vegan cookbook at the café, downloading geeky fiction e-books, or digging new music and timely videos from our website.

PM Press is always on the lookout for talented and skilled volunteers, artists, activists, and writers to work with. If you have a great idea for a project or can contribute in some way, please get in touch.

PM Press
PO Box 23912
Oakland, CA 94623
www.pmpress.org

FRIENDS OF PM PRESS

These are indisputably momentous times—the financial system is melting down globally and the Empire is stumbling. Now more than ever there is a vital need for radical ideas.

In the years since its founding—and on a mere shoestring—PM Press has risen to the formidable challenge of publishing and distributing knowledge and entertainment for the struggles ahead. With over 300 releases to date, we have published an impressive and stimulating array of literature, art, music, politics, and culture. Using every available medium, we've succeeded in connecting those hungry for ideas and information to those putting them into practice.

Friends of PM allows you to directly help impact, amplify, and revitalize the discourse and actions of radical writers, filmmakers, and artists. It provides us with a stable foundation from which we can build upon our early successes and provides a much-needed subsidy for the materials that can't necessarily pay their own way. You can help make that happen—and receive every new title automatically delivered to your door once a month—by joining as a Friend of PM Press. And, we'll throw in a free T-shirt when you sign up.

Here are your options:

- **$30 a month** Get all books and pamphlets plus 50% discount on all webstore purchases

- **$40 a month** Get all PM Press releases (including CDs and DVDs) plus 50% discount on all webstore purchases

- **$100 a month** Superstar—Everything plus PM merchandise, free downloads, and 50% discount on all webstore purchases

For those who can't afford $30 or more a month, we're introducing **Sustainer Rates** at $15, $10 and $5. Sustainers get a free PM Press T-shirt and a 50% discount on all purchases from our website.

Your Visa or Mastercard will be billed once a month, until you tell us to stop. Or until our efforts succeed in bringing the revolution around. Or the financial meltdown of Capital makes plastic redundant. Whichever comes first.

Anthropocene or Capitalocene? Nature, History, and the Crisis of Capitalism

Edited by Jason W. Moore

ISBN: 978-1-62963-148-6
$21.95   304 pages

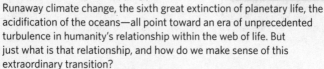

The Earth has reached a tipping point. Runaway climate change, the sixth great extinction of planetary life, the acidification of the oceans—all point toward an era of unprecedented turbulence in humanity's relationship within the web of life. But just what is that relationship, and how do we make sense of this extraordinary transition?

Anthropocene or Capitalocene? offers answers to these questions from a dynamic group of leading critical scholars. They challenge the theory and history offered by the most significant environmental concept of our times: the Anthropocene. But are we living in the Anthropocene, literally the "Age of Man"? Is a different response more compelling, and better suited to the strange—and often terrifying—times in which we live? The contributors to this book diagnose the problems of Anthropocene thinking and propose an alternative: the global crises of the twenty-first century are rooted in the Capitalocene; not the Age of Man but the Age of Capital.

Anthropocene or Capitalocene? offers a series of provocative essays on nature and power, humanity, and capitalism. Including both well-established voices and younger scholars, the book challenges the conventional practice of dividing historical change and contemporary reality into "Nature" and "Society," demonstrating the possibilities offered by a more nuanced and connective view of human environment-making, joined at every step with and within the biosphere. In distinct registers, the authors frame their discussions within a politics of hope that signal the possibilities for transcending capitalism, broadly understood as a "world-ecology" that joins nature, capital, and power as a historically evolving whole.

Contributors include Jason W. Moore, Eileen Crist, Donna J. Haraway, Andreas Malm, Elmar Altvater, Daniel Hartley, and Christian Parenti.

Birth Work as Care Work: Stories from Activist Birth Communities

Alana Apfel, with a foreword by Loretta J. Ross, preface by Victoria Law, and introduction by Silvia Federici

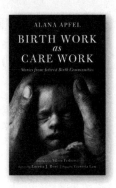

ISBN: 978-1-62963-151-6
$14.95   128 pages

Birth Work as Care Work presents a vibrant collection of stories and insights from the front lines of birth activist communities. The personal has once more become political, and birth workers, supporters, and doulas now find themselves at the fore of collective struggles for freedom and dignity.

The author, herself a scholar and birth justice organiser, provides a unique platform to explore the political dynamics of birth work; drawing connections between birth, reproductive labor, and the struggles of caregiving communities today. Articulating a politics of care work in and through the reproductive process, the book brings diverse voices into conversation to explore multiple possibilities and avenues for change.

At a moment when agency over our childbirth experiences is increasingly centralized in the hands of professional elites, *Birth Work as Care Work* presents creative new ways to reimagine the trajectory of our reproductive processes. Most importantly, the contributors present new ways of thinking about the entire life cycle, providing a unique and creative entry point into the essence of all human struggle—the struggle over the reproduction of life itself.

"I love this book, all of it. The polished essays and the interviews with birth workers dare to take on the deepest questions of human existence."
—Carol Downer, cofounder of the Feminist Women's Heath Centers of California and author of *A Woman's Book of Choices*

"This volume provides theoretically rich, practical tools for birth and other care workers to collectively and effectively fight capitalism and the many intersecting processes of oppression that accompany it. Birth Work as Care Work *forcefully and joyfully reminds us that the personal is political, a lesson we need now more than ever."*
—Adrienne Pine, author of *Working Hard, Drinking Hard: On Violence and Survival in Honduras*

From SPECTRE from PM Press

Capital and Its Discontents: Conversations with Radical Thinkers in a Time of Tumult

Sasha Lilley

ISBN: 978-1-60486-334-5
$20.00   320 pages

Capitalism is stumbling, empire is faltering, and the planet is thawing. Yet many people are still grasping to understand these multiple crises and to find a way forward to a just future. Into the breach come the essential insights of *Capital and Its Discontents*, which cut through the gristle to get to the heart of the matter about the nature of capitalism and imperialism, capitalism's vulnerabilities at this conjuncture—and what can we do to hasten its demise. Through a series of incisive conversations with some of the most eminent thinkers and political economists on the Left—including David Harvey, Ellen Meiksins Wood, Mike Davis, Leo Panitch, Tariq Ali, and Noam Chomsky—*Capital and Its Discontents* illuminates the dynamic contradictions undergirding capitalism and the potential for its dethroning. At a moment when capitalism as a system is more reviled than ever, here is an indispensable toolbox of ideas for action by some of the most brilliant thinkers of our times.

"*These conversations illuminate the current world situation in ways that are very useful for those hoping to orient themselves and find a way forward to effective individual and collective action. Highly recommended.*"
—Kim Stanley Robinson, *New York Times* bestselling author of the *Mars Trilogy* and *The Years of Rice and Salt*

"*In this fine set of interviews, an A-list of radical political economists demonstrate why their skills are indispensable to understanding today's multiple economic and ecological crises.*"
—Raj Patel, author of *Stuffed and Starved* and *The Value of Nothing*

"*This is an extremely important book. It is the most detailed, comprehensive, and best study yet published on the most recent capitalist crisis and its discontents. Sasha Lilley sets each interview in its context, writing with style, scholarship, and wit about ideas and philosophies.*"
—Andrej Grubačić, radical sociologist and social critic, co-author of *Wobblies and Zapatistas*